# Superstars
## of
## Country Music

# Also by Gene Busnar

*Careers in Music*
*It's Rock 'N' Roll*
*Superstars of Rock*

# Superstars of Country Music

## Gene Busnar

JULIAN MESSNER  NEW YORK

Copyright © 1984 by Eugene Busnar

All rights reserved including the right of
reproduction in whole or in part in any form.
Published by Julian Messner,
A Division of Simon & Schuster, Inc.
Simon & Schuster Building,
1230 Avenue of the Americas,
New York, New York 10020.
JULIAN MESSNER and colophon are trademarks of Simon & Schuster, Inc.

10 9 8 7 6 5 4 3 2 1

Design by Teresa Delgado, A Good Thing, Inc.
Picture Credits: Columbia Records, pg. 36; *Record World,* pgs. 8, 62, 76,
105, 107, 126, 144, 154, 184, 205; Mark Rothbaum Agency/CBS Records, pg. 92; RCA Records, pg. 120; Ken Kragen Management, pgs.
162, 179; Brokaw Gangwisch Public Relations/Epic Records, pg. 214.


Library of Congress Cataloging in Publication Data
Busnar, Gene.
   Superstars of country music.

   Bibliography: p.
   Includes index.
   1. Country musicians—United States—Biography.
I. Title.
ML385.B965   1984      784.5′2′00922 [B]   83-23842
ISBN 0-671-45627-X

For Elizabeth

Acknowledgments

I would like to thank the following for their help: *Record World* magazine; Mark Rothbaum; Cynthia Lew of Columbia Records in Nashville; Jerry Flowers and Randy Goodman of RCA Records in Nashville; Mary Ann Luther of Brokaw-Gangwisch Public Relations; Jerry Baily, MCA Records in Nashville; Ken Kragen and his entire staff; Ronnie Pegh of the Country Music Foundation Library and Media Center. Special thanks to Cathy Anagnostakis, Pauline Walker, and Coleen Cool for their help in researching this book; my wife Liz for her work on the Collector's Guides; and my editor Iris Rosoff for her patience and expertise. Special thanks to Amy Kaplan for the discography.

# Contents

Hank Williams in 1952—
the king of country music.

*I just make music the way I know how. Singin' songs come natural to me the way some folks can argue law or make cabinets. It's all I know. It's all I care about.*
*Hank Williams in an interview with Melvin Shestack*

As the most influential performer in modern country music, Hank Williams has been the subject of books, articles, and controversies of one kind or another for the past thirty years. But how much is really known about the man? As far as anyone can tell, Hank Williams granted only two extended interviews during his short but illustrious career: one to journalist Ralph J. Gleason and the other to a high-school reporter named Melvin Shestack. His most famous quote is a description of country music in a magazine called *Nation's Business*: "(Country music) can be explained in just one word," Williams proclaimed. "Sincerity."

*When a hillbilly sings a crazy song, he feels crazy. When he sings "I laid my mother away," he sees her a layin' right there in the coffin. He sings more sincere than most entertainers because the hillbilly was raised rougher than most entertainers. You got to know a lot about hard work. You got to have smelled a lot of mule manure before you can sing like a hillbilly. The people who have been raised something like the way a hillbilly has know what he is singing about and appreciate it.*

Hank Williams had a knack for writing and singing songs that had the qualities which he spoke about in that article. In certain respects, it would be fair to call Hank Williams a genius. He seemed to have an instinct for creating music that reached not only the "hillbillies" of the rural South, but the much larger national, or "popular," audience. In a very real sense, he shaped the country sound for decades to come and laid the groundwork for the growing recognition that country artists are currently receiving throughout the world.

It is not always easy to appreciate an artist's genius years after the fact. Most of today's younger country music fans have heard the results of Hank Williams's influence, but how many are familiar with Hank's own records? That is one of the problems in appreciating any kind of popular music. The word *popular* relates to what is happening today, *right now.* Only in recent years have people begun to concern themselves with the roots of the songs that are popular. From that point of view, it would be fair to say that without Hank Williams, country music would have a far different character than it does today. It is also very possible that without Hank Williams, there might never have been the kind of rock and roll originated by Elvis Presley only a few short years after Williams's untimely death.

But what of Hank Williams the man? When someone is labeled a genius and an innovator, it is natural for people to want to know about that person. And if they come to relate to that person's music, people also want to believe that the individual was someone they would have liked to know. In reality, great musical ability seems to have little or nothing to do with how a performer leads his or her life or relates to other people. There are not very many established facts about Hank Williams the man, but we do know that he wasn't a very strong person. His life is often referred to as a tragedy. Of course, it is always a tragedy when anyone dies at the age of twenty-nine. It is particularly tragic, though, when that person is talented, rich, and idolized by millions of adoring fans.

## Beginnings

Hiram Hank Williams was born on September 17, 1923, near a small town called Georgiana, Alabama, some sixty miles from Montgomery. Perhaps the most remarkable thing about his birth was an unsightly sore at the base of his spine. Some people say Hank's abuse of alcohol and drugs, and his untimely death, may have had something to do with his painful birth defect. Hank's father Lonnie was a poor sharecropper who also worked as a locomotive-driver and ran logging rigs. Lonnie had fought in World War I, and, apparently, that experience had left him with a variety of health problems that eventually landed him in a Veteran's Administration hospital. Lilly, Hank's mother, was a strong, domineering woman who often criticized her husband for his inability to provide a better living for her and her two children, six-year-old Irene and baby Hiram. When Hank was seven, Lonnie's health deteriorated. He checked into the V.A. hospital in Biloxi, Mississippi. There are some who claim that Lilly gave Hank's dad such a hard time that life in the hospital may have provided him with a good measure of relief.

Lilly Williams was a tower of strength in every respect. Six feet tall and over two hundred pounds, she cut an imposing physical presence. As aggressive in business as she was big in size, Lilly found a large house and rented out the extra rooms to boarders. The children were sent out to work while their mother stayed home and tended her new venture.

In *Sing a Sad Song, The Life of Hank Williams*, author Roger Williams describes Hank's first job selling peanuts and shining shoes:

*Irene roasted some peanuts and put them in little paper bags. Hank took them out on the streets of Georgiana. He also took a can of shoe polish and a rag, and anyone passing up the peanuts was offered a shine instead. Each sold for a nickel. No one recalls just how good of a seller or shiner Hank was, but by the end of the day he had made thirty cents. With (that money), he bought stew meat and rice, potatoes and tomatoes. He pre-*

*sented the food triumphantly to his mother and exclaimed, "Momma, fix us some gumbo stew. We're gonna eat tonight!"*

The young boy with his peanuts and shoeshine kit became a fixture in the small town. Jay Caress, author of *Hank Williams: Country Music's Tragic King*, feels that because Hank had no father, he relied on what he learned on the streets as a model for "how to talk, how to view the world, and how he might be able to earn a living." Hank didn't have a particularly happy childhood. No one could ever measure what effect the absence of his father had on the youngster.

Perhaps the most important and, in some ways, the happiest year of Hank's boyhood was when he went to live with his cousin J. C. McNeil. The McNeils were not as poor as Hank's family and Walter McNeil—J. C.'s father—took a liking to the eleven-year-old Hank. It was during his year with the McNeils that Hank got his first real taste of two things that would shape his life—alcohol and country music.

On Saturday nights, the men who worked the logging camps and the local farmers would gather. From a nearby bush, Hank and his cousin J. C. could hear the music and see couples dancing. Both Lilly and J. C.'s mother were religious women, who made their children attend church every Sunday. But the music and the laughter the boys were listening to now were unlike anything one hears in a church. *These people weren't praying, they were having fun.* When the two young onlookers were finally discovered, they were invited to join the festivities. Before long, Hank was sipping his first shot of hard liquor.

To have tasted liquor at such an early age was not in itself so unusual for that time and place. Many young boys who had similar experiences did not become alcoholics, but Hank was different. Aside from the sadness he felt about growing up without a father, Hank had witnessed the heavy drinking his dad had indulged in before checking into the V.A. Hospital. It is also possible that Hank's birth defect caused him physical pain from which alcohol provided welcome relief. Whatever the reasons, Hank had started a habit that would ultimately help kill him. In his book, *Your Cheatin' Heart,* author Chet Flippo imagines what young Hank (Hiram) must have experienced after swallowing that first drink:

> *He felt a warm flush spread through his body and he suddenly felt bigger and everything around him took on a hard glow. He no longer felt tense and his head felt light. The flames were dancing and the music was louder and he suddenly seemed to . . . understand a lot of things. He and J. C. started dancing, skipping back and forth while the men laughed and egged them on. Hiram got dizzy and fell over on his back in the red dust. He was laughing, though, and felt wonderful. He didn't*

*feel ordinary anymore. He didn't hear the loggers laughing at the drunk kid. He felt special.*

If you read about people who have trouble handling fame and fortune, you may notice that indulging in too much alcohol is often part of their behavior. Some of them manage to straighten out their lives before it is too late, but Hank wasn't so fortunate. Because of his unhappy childhood, it is possible that the feeling he had after that first drunken night was better and stronger than any he had ever felt before. Perhaps that is why he may have never even seriously thought about stopping what soon became an uncontrollable habit.

Hank's interest in music was also fueled by his experiences while living with the McNeils. Those same shindigs where Hank first tasted bootleg corn whiskey were also the places where he first heard live country music. It is thought that Mrs. McNeil showed Hank how to play his first basic guitar chords. In any event, when Hank returned to his mother's house in Georgiana, he showed a keen interest in music.

Shortly after Hank's return, Lilly moved the family to nearby Greenville, where she ran another boarding house. Hank resumed his peanut selling and shoe-shining. As far as Lilly was concerned, her son's life was much as it was before his year with the McNeils.

But the young boy was staying in town much later now, hanging out with a slight, gray-haired black street singer nicknamed Tee-Tot. Hank followed Tee-Tot through the streets of Greenville as he sang his songs and passed the hat.

Now that his interest in music had grown, young Hank made it a point on his shoe-shine and peanut rounds to pass all the places where he could get a taste of the different musical styles that attracted him. He listened and spoke with the white guitarists and fiddlers who sat around and exchanged traditional folk songs. But he was even more fascinated by the shuffling rhythms and moaning blues that he picked up from hanging out in the black section of town.

Although Hank's mother did not approve of her son following a black street singer around, she was impressed enough with his intense interest in music to agree to buy him a secondhand guitar. Although he never became a great guitar player, Hank learned the strong, simple rhythms he needed to accompany his rapidly developing singing powers. From Tee-Tot Hank also learned how to work a crowd. Jay Caress explains the relationship between mentor (Tee-Tot) and student (Hank) this way:

*Neither (Hank nor Tee-Tot) was inclined toward the kind of gut-busting, survival-wage jobs that characterized the southern work-market in the thirties; neither of them was on the "inside" of Alabama society, and neither knew or cared about the simple pleasures of domestic (life). That left young Hank Williams and Tee-Tot with their guitars, with feet that . . . itched to tap out a beat, and with a kind of . . . longing to be heard and understood . . . soul brothers to be sure.*

*And the elder brother . . . passed on to his student the tools Hank needed to forge his strengths and talents into a career. . . Tee-Tot's entire style was based on the grim fact that he rarely had a captive audience; he had to be able to stop people on the sidewalk, to grab 'em with an infectious delivery, to (rivet) 'em with bold, frank eye contact, and to pull 'em along with the rhythm of a boogie beat thumped out of an unamplified guitar. Furthermore, he had to keep his audience for at least two or three songs, so they'd feel they owed him something, something they'd drop into his hat before they went on about their business. . . .*

*(Hank) knew what kind of hunger put ol' Tee-Tot out there on the streets day after day. He knew what the blues was already—from the inside out—and he knew, just as a spawning salmon knows how to swim upstream, that he had found his own quest.*

When Hank was almost fourteen, Lilly moved the family to the much larger city of Montgomery. The city had two large country radio stations, and Hank felt ready to try his hand at the music business. He had learned more in his two years on the streets of Greenville than some men learn in a lifetime. Tee-Tot had shown him most of the guitar chords and tricks of the trade that he would need to become a professional entertainer. Hank still had to attend school. But as far as he was concerned, the lessons he had learned from Tee-Tot were the only ones that really mattered.

## "The Singing Kid"

One of Lilly's reasons for moving to Montgomery may well have been to separate Hank from Tee-Tot and to discourage his fascination with music. But the fourteen-year-old Hank understood that the move offered a real chance to make his dreams come true. Montgomery was a small music center in its own right. Aside from the two radio stations—whose signals were picked up hundreds of miles away—there were several theaters that featured country music and dozens of small clubs where young musicians could cut their teeth. Lilly was still sending Hank out with his peanuts and shoe-shine kit, but he was crafty enough to start hanging out in and around the two radio stations.

A few short months after his arrival in Montgomery, Hank felt confident enough to walk into the studios of radio station WCOV and ask for a chance to sing. The person Hank approached was a singer named Braxton Schuffert. Only eighteen himself, Schuffert already had his own shows on both radio stations. This wasn't the first time some starstruck kid had asked him for help. More often than not, these were young people whose dreams were far greater than their musical talents. Still, something about Hank appealed to Schuffert, and he invited the boy to come out to the club where his band was working that night and sit in. Schuffert was impressed with Hank's singing and suggested that he enter a local Saturday-night talent contest.

Hank didn't need to be asked twice. He put on his best cowboy clothes and had no doubt that he would win the fifteen-dollar prize. This would be the push he needed to become a full-fledged professional singer. The song he sang that night was an original composition, called "WPA Blues." He may have been nervous when he hit the stage, but no one could tell as he belted out the words:

*I got a home in Montgomery*
*A place I like to stay.*
*But I have to work for the WPA,*
*And I'm dissatisfied—I'm dissatisfied.*

Hank Williams definitely struck a chord in the audience that night. He was the hands-down winner of the talent show. Within a few short weeks, he became a regular feature on a radio show that starred Dad Crysell's Band. It seemed only natural to give Hank the nickname, "The Singing Kid." From there, Hank got his own radio show. "He was on his way," Jay Caress wrote. "Just turned fourteen, (and) he was appearing twice a week on the biggest country music station in Alabama."

On his radio show, Hank sang and accompanied himself on guitar. He knew, though, that he needed a band if he was going to become a major star. At first, he teamed up with another young singer named Hezzy Adair. Hank and Hezzy was what they called themselves. But Hank had no intention of sharing the top billing. It wasn't long until the name of the band was changed to Hank Williams and the Drifting Cowboys. Although there were many personnel changes over the years, the name stuck throughout Hank's career.

Some of the most notorious Hank Williams's stories come out of his first years working small bars throughout southern Alabama. These bars were tough. The hard-working men who visited the honky-tonks where Hank and the Drifting Cowboys worked sometimes liked to blow off a little steam after they got a few stiff drinks under their belts. Sometimes things would get more than a little rowdy, and before long, Hank became quite a barroom fighter himself. Musicians who worked with him recall that Hank was right in the middle of many a free-for-all. Often his greatest ally in these battles was his mother.

Lilly Williams was no fool when it came to business. By this time she realized that the young boy who used to follow black street singers around town was now capable of generating some fairly serious money. Lilly appointed herself the band's driver, manager, and money collector. It is said that she was without equal in the toughest barroom fights. She also wasn't beyond punching Hank out when he got drunk and seemed likely to squander all his money. "Hank was ready for any comers," Chet Flippo observes, "except his mother."

By the time he reached his late teens, Hank had established himself as the best country singer in Alabama. He was completely at ease when on a stage, and equally at home joking with the audience as singing. But Hank had also developed a reputation as an unreliable drunk. Apparently, he could go through fairly long periods without drinking. But like many others with a similar problem, once he started there was no stopping him. As legend has it, a band member asked Hank if he'd like a beer, to which he replied: "Old Hank doesn't have just one beer." The dual reputation that Hank developed as a giant talent with enormous personal problems is one that stuck with him to the bitter end.

In 1942, Hank met Audrey Mae Sheppard Guy, a woman who was to become even more instrumental to his career than his mother. When Hank took Audrey home to meet his mother, a tremendous fight took place. Apparently, Lilly sensed that Audrey was still married. She pulled Hank aside and told him what she thought of his new girl. Perhaps Lilly could tell that Audrey was someone who could get Hank to do what *she* wanted him to do. Where would that leave the mother who had worked so hard helping her boy become the big local star he now was?

Audrey made no secret of the fact that she was married at the time to a serviceman who was fighting overseas. But she planned to get a divorce as soon as possible. She figured that between Hank's talent and her ambition, they could go far. She was also under the false impression that she was a musical talent in her own right—she was actually an awful singer. Still, Hank was so crazy about Audrey that he often let her sing with the Drifting Cowboys. Later on, when he was the hottest performer in country music, Hank still had to contend with Audrey's insistence that he feature her as part of his act. But during those years, Audrey's farfetched singing ambitions were only part of his problem. Once the two of them got married, the battle between wife and mother reached new heights, as did Hank's drinking.

People outside of Alabama had heard about Hank. Even his two greatest singing idols—Ernest Tubb and Roy Acuff—had come to check him out. Tubb recommended that the Grand Ole Opry—country music's most highly regarded road show—give Hank a shot. But the folks who managed the Opry knew about Hank's drunken binges and, in spite of his talent, they decided not to add him to the show. What that meant, in effect, was that Hank was not able to move out of the minor leagues. Not yet, anyway.

## On to Nashville

Audrey had no intention of settling for the small-time honky tonks and medicine shows that Hank was stuck in. She was in this for the big time, and that meant Nashville. There was no doubt in her mind that Hank had the talent to become a big star. What he needed was the right management, and she was the one to help him get it. In those days, the best management in Nashville was Acuff-Rose. And in the late summer of 1946, that's exactly where Audrey and Hank headed.

Fred Rose had established himself as a songwriter and vaudeville performer during the twenties and thirties. After writing a number of hits for Roy Acuff, the two started their own music publishing company and had built up an impressive roster of hit country songwriters. When a tall, skinny fellow and his attractive wife walked into their offices in 1946, Acuff-Rose could hardly have guessed that this man would evolve into their most important talent.

Fred Rose and his son Wesley were playing a game of ping-pong during their lunch hour when Audrey Williams walked in and asked that they listen to her husband sing. Today, if an unknown person tried to walk into a major publishing office without an appointment, he or she would be promptly shown the exit door. Even in the forties, it was highly irregular for someone to barge in and actually get heard. Nevertheless, Fred Rose decided to listen to the tall, shy fellow who mumbled that his name was Hank Williams.

Hank hadn't planned what songs he was going to sing. He really never believed that the great Fred Rose would just let him walk in and sing. The three songs Hank sang were: "When God Comes and Gathers His Jewels," "My Love For You (Has Turned To Hate)," and "Six More Miles to the Graveyard." Within a matter of minutes, Fred Rose offered Hank a publishing contract. As lucky as Hank thought he was at that moment, he could not have possibly understood the extent of his good fortune.

Although the relationships between songwriters and music publishers are somewhat better today, songwriters still get exploited all the time. When a song is recorded, the writer is supposed to receive a royalty on the sale of sheet music and records, and each time the song is played on the radio. However, many a songwriter who is short on cash has sold a future hit song for a hundred, fifty, and even ten dollars.

It is likely that Fred Rose could have exploited Hank to the hilt. But Fred Rose was not that kind of man. On the contrary, he helped Hank write many of his songs and refused to take any of the credit. Of course, he owned the copyright on the songs, and knew he would make his share of money that way. Still, he treated Hank more like a son and a friend than like a businessman. When all is said and done, Fred Rose might have been one of Hank's only friends.

When Hank and Audrey walked out of the Rose-Acuff offices on that afternoon in 1946, Hank was feeling happier than he could ever remember. Here he had been writing songs for years without making a dime on them, and now the great Fred Rose wanted to pay him for them. In sharp contrast, Audrey was not happy at all. She was hoping that Hank would get a record deal so they could move to Nashville immediately. As it stood, they had to return to Alabama and wait a while longer.

# Hank the Recording Artist

Even the ambitious Audrey was surprised when only six months after their first trip to Nashville, Fred Rose called to say that he had secured some recording work for Hank on the small Sterling record label. There was no contract beyond the four original songs Hank recorded for a flat fee of ninety dollars. Aaron Shelton, who engineered the recording session, was moved by Hank's songs. But he saw even more potential in Hank as a performer. "The pure magnetism of the guy's presentation is what (I) couldn't help but notice," Shelton told Jay Caress.

At first, the owners of Sterling Records were not especially impressed with Hank. But the recordings sold rather well, and they promptly booked him for a second recording session. One of the songs Hank cut then was "Honky-Tonkin'," a tune that was to establish his style of upbeat, fun-loving, blues-based songs. This style was used on Hank's first major hit record, "Lovesick Blues," two years later. Fred Rose knew when he heard "Honky-Tonkin'" that it was time to hook Hank up with a major record label. There was no doubt in Rose's mind now that Hank had the qualities to reach the top of the country music world.

Fred Rose played the Sterling cuts for the owner of the new MGM record label in New York, and a short time later Hank was signed to his first major recording contract. It was that same Fred Rose—whom Hank affectionately called "Pappy"—who guided Hank through every stage of his career. Not only did Rose help Hank make his songs more commercial and secure the best record deals, he supervised every one of Hank's recording sessions and guided his performing career.

Hank's first release on MGM was "Move It On Over." The song sold several hundred thousand records and established Hank as a hit recording artist. However, Fred Rose understood that if Hank was to reach his potential as a major star, he had to be seen as well as heard. Rose would have preferred booking Hank with the Grand Ole Opry. But because of Hank's reputation as a drinker and a brawler, the Opry's management was in no hurry to sign him on. Rose decided that the next best radio show/touring company to set Hank up with would be Shreveport's Louisiana Hayride. Hank needed a proving ground as a performer, and Rose felt the Hayride would be just the right setting. He would also be handled by the Hayride's live booking services and would finally be able to tour like a professional country performer. The performers would be booked out on the road all week, but Saturday nights they would have to be back in Shreveport to do the Louisiana Hayride over radio station KWKH. Hank felt confident that if things worked out on the Hayride, he would soon be called up to the major leagues of country music—the Grand Ole Opry.

Hank still had one major problem that was holding up his career—alcohol. He knew, as did everyone who worked with him, that his ability to control his drinking was now the big issue in how far he would go. Hank was an alcoholic, there was no question about that. The question was whether he could keep himself sober long enough to make a name as a dependable, star-quality, performer. According to those who were around him at the time, Hank managed to stay away from the bottle during most of his stay at Shreveport.

Aside from becoming the Hayride's major attraction, Hank also had his own radio show on station KWKH, sponsored by Johnny Fair Syrup. Hank's singing and down-home conversation made him the perfect salesman for the product. He called himself the "Old Syrup Sopper," and soon became one of the station's most popular radio personalities. On Saturday nights on the Hayride, Hank perfected his stage act. "He was just electrifying on stage," KWKH's Frank Page told author Roger Williams. "He had the people in the palm of his hands from the moment he walked out there. They were with him, whatever he wanted to do."

Jay Caress describes Hank's performance this way:

*When introduced, Hank Williams would . . . slouch out to the microphone, but as soon as the music began, it was off to the races. . . . His body moved with the music, the cowboy-booted toes tapping and the long legs bending with the rhythms. On the fast numbers, Hank began to bounce and bob like a boxer, all the while holding his audience spellbound with the intensity of his eyes. Those dark, sad expressive eyes flickered with fun or they pleaded with the sad songs, but they seemed always to shine with life.*

*Meanwhile, of course, Hank was singing. And somehow . . . it was as if there had never been anybody else (singing) a country song. This is what country music sounded like. Everything else was just an imitation of this original. Haven't we heard this voice before? It's so* familar. *But where?*

The truth of the matter is that like any other performer Hank had his influences. By his own admission he idolized Jimmy Rodgers, Roy Acuff, and Ernest Tubb. When he started out, he was trying for a sound somewhere between Acuff and Tubb. But as he developed, the sound and his performance style became totally his own. Whether it was on up-tempo numbers like "Jambalaya," "Move It On Over," and "Lovesick Blues," or slow tear-jerkers like "Cold Cold Heart," "Your Cheatin' Heart," or "I'm So Lonesome I Could Cry," Hank reached the people as no country music performer ever had. Hank was also one of the first country songwriters to pen a hit song for a popular performer. Tony Bennett—the great pop-jazz singer—had a national hit with "Cold Cold Heart," and proved that some country songs could reach people who didn't live in the South.

Hank's growing acclaim, however, did little to ease his personal problems. Hank's success was so great that even the powers at the Grand Ole Opry finally had to give in and invite him to perform. "Lovesick Blues" had become just too big a hit to keep Hank off the Opry stage. Roger Williams describes that debut on June 11, 1949, one that ranks as the most memorable in that show's history:

> *A wildly cheering audience brought him back a half-dozen times to sing the closing line of "Lovesick Blues": "I'm lo-o-onesome, I got the lovesick blues." Master of ceremonies Red Foley had to plead with the crowd to cease howling for more and let the program proceed. Nothing could stop Hank Williams after that, except himself. In the (next) three years, he rose to and fell from the (peak) of country music success. Six months later, he was dead.*

## His Legacy

While Hank was turning out his records under his own name, he also recorded some other sides under the name Luke the Drifter. These songs were too sad,

Fred Rose felt, to be released as Hank Williams's records. It is in some of these songs that we can glimpse the depths of pain that Hank Williams lived with. In one song, "Men with Broken Hearts," Luke (Hank) speaks of brokenhearted men like himself who "live within the past." He reminds us that we cannot know such pain unless we've gone through this "living death" ourselves. Perhaps Hank was trying to give his listeners some kind of explanation of why someone who seemingly had the world by the tail counted himself among the brokenhearted people of this world.

Hank's death on New Year's Day of 1953 was a day of mourning for his many fans. It is not clear to what extent alcohol and drugs were involved in the performer's death. The point was that country music's biggest and brightest star was dead. The occasion called for the largest and most publicized funeral the South had ever seen. About 25,000 people lined the streets of Montgomery to pay their respects. Inside, other country music greats like Roy Acuff, Ernest Tubb, and Red Foley sang spirituals and religious hymns.

Aside from the mourning and respect that Hank's death produced, it also spawned a new industry—the I Remember Hank Williams Industry. Countless memorial records by imitators were released. Unfinished tapes were touched up and put on the market. Hank had taken a second wife—Billy Jean—after Audrey divorced him, and both women had gone on the road billed as "Mrs. Hank Williams." There was even a Hollywood movie made in the sixties—*Your Cheatin' Heart*—featuring the singing of Hank Williams, Jr. (Hank and Audrey's only son). Hank had never bothered to make out a will, so the distribution of his estate was disputed for many years, with Hank's mother and two wives the main contestants.

But what is the real legacy of Hank Williams? He is still one of country music's most imitated performers. His songs are played on juke boxes across the land: his own versions and those of performers beginning with Ray Charles and ending with the Lawrence Welk Orchestra. His life and untimely death are just one more in a seemingly endless series of lessons that success in show business has nothing at all to do with personal happiness. Perhaps Chet Flippo sums it up best on the last page of his book, *Your Cheatin' Heart*:

*The man wrote hardly any letters, read nothing but comic books, and revealed his inner self only through his songs. Those who did know him revise his history to sweeten their own. Plain facts and dates do not explain him or his extraordinary impact on American music and particularly on whole generations in the South.*

# Hank Williams Collector's Guide

| ALBUM | LABEL (all albums recorded by MGM) |
|---|---|
| Greatest Hits | |
| Greatest Hits Volume II | |
| Greatest Hits Volume III | |
| The Very Best of Hank Williams | |
| The Very Best of Hank Williams Volume II | |
| Father and Son | |
| Hank Williams, Sr. and Hank Williams, Jr. | |
| Hank Williams Sings "Kaw-Linga" and Other Humorous Songs | |
| The Legend Lives Anew | |
| Luke the Drifter | |
| Immortal (Metro) | |
| In the Beginning | |
| The Essential Hank Williams | |
| 24-Karat Hits | |
| 24 of Hank Williams's Greatest Hits | |
| Williams in Song and Story | |

# Hank Williams Collector's Guide

| YEAR | SINGLE | LABEL | C&W | POP |
|---|---|---|---|---|
| 1946 | Never Again Will I Knock | MGM | | |
| 1947 | Honky Tonkin' | MGM | | |
| 1948 | Move It On Over | MGM | | |
| 1949 | Lovesick Blues | MGM | * | |
| 1949 | Wedding Bells | MGM | * | |
| 1949 | Mind Your Own Business | MGM | * | |
| 1949 | You're Gonna Change | MGM | * | |
| 1949 | Lost Highway | MGM | | |

| YEAR | SINGLE | LABEL | C&W | POP |
|------|--------|-------|-----|-----|
| 1949 | My Pocket's Got a Hole in It | MGM | | * |
| 1950 | I Just Don't Like This Kind of Livin' | MGM | | * |
| 1950 | Long Gone Lonesome Blues | MGM | | * |
| 1950 | Why Don't You Love Me | MGM | | * |
| 1950 | Why Should We Try Anymore | MGM | | * |
| 1950 | Moaning the Blues | MGM | | * |
| 1951 | Dear John | MGM | | * |
| 1951 | Cold Cold Heart | MGM | | * |
| 1951 | Howlin' at the Moon | MGM | | * |
| 1951 | I Can't Help It | MGM | | * |
| 1951 | Hey Good Lookin' | MGM | | * |
| 1951 | Crazy Heart | MGM | | * |
| 1951 | Baby We're Really in Love | MGM | | * |
| 1952 | Honky-Tonk Blues | MGM | | * |
| 1952 | Half as Much | MGM | | * |
| 1952 | Jambalaya | MGM | | * |
| 1952 | Settin' the Woods on Fire | MGM | | * |
| 1952 | I'll Never Get Out of this World Alive | MGM | | * |
| 1953 | Kaw-Linga | MGM | | * |
| 1953 | Your Cheatin' Heart | MGM | | * |
| 1953 | Take Those Chains from My Heart | MGM | | * |
| 1953 | I Won't Be Home No More | MGM | | * |
| 1953 | Weary Blues from Waitin' | MGM | | * |
| 1966 | I'm So Lonesome I Could Cry | MGM | | |

*Smash Hit

Johnny Cash—"man in black."

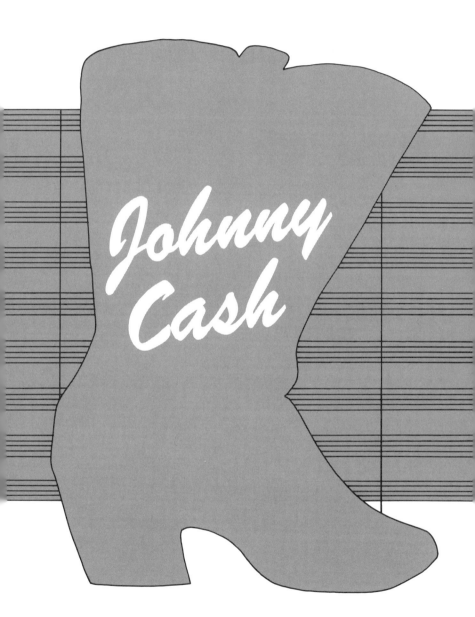

*If it is possible in this modern era for one to be of folk origin, then Johnny Cash definitely meets the requirements.*
                              *Bill Malone,* Country Music U.S.A.

There is a lot of talk about country performers "crossing over" into rock, but this is nothing new. Back in the early fifties, a man named Sam Phillips was looking for a "white singer with a black feel" to record on his Memphis-based Sun record label. Phillips was certain that his success in discovering such a talent would earn him a million dollars.

In 1953, a young truck driver named Elvis Presley dropped by the Sun studios to make a record as a birthday present for his mother. Phillip's secretary thought that Elvis might be the singer her boss had been searching for. She was right. Like other talented young singers in that part of the country, Elvis had grown up with a feeling for the blues, pop songs, religious hymns, and authentic country music. It was simply a question of Phillips helping Elvis find a style that was both original and commercial.

After Elvis's phenomenal success, singers from all over the South bombarded Phillips with tapes and requests for live auditions. Needless to say, the majority of these performers never got a record contract. But Phillips discovered that some of the young, would-be stars actually were diamonds in the rough.

The stars whom Phillips helped launch included: Jerry Lee Lewis, that wild piano man who recorded "Great Balls of Fire" and "Whole Lot of Shakin' Goin' On;" Carl Perkins, who recorded "Blue Suede Shoes" before Elvis; Roy Orbison; Charlie Rich; and a tall, slow-talking man from Arkansas named Johnny Cash.

When Johnny Cash and his band—the Tennessee Two—first visited Sun Records in March 1955, they did not generate much enthusiasm. The sound Sam Phillips wanted had to be similar to the excitement and urgency that Elvis projected. When Cash presented a few original gospel hymns in that low-keyed, conversational style that has become his trademark, Phillips's only response was: "I love gospel songs, too, John . . . but we have to sell records to stay in business." A few months later, Cash and the Tennessee Two showed up at Sun's Union Avenue studios again. This time, though, they had worked up a few songs in a more commercial vein, and Phillips came across with a recording contract.

Johnny's first country hit was "Cry, Cry, Cry." This was followed by "So Doggone Lonesome," "Get Rhythm," and "Folsom Prison Blues." But it wasn't until the release of "I Walk the Line" in 1956 that Johnny logged his first national top-ten hit. This was soon followed by a number of spots on network television. From there, Johnny Cash's career took off. In the years to come, he would sell tens of millions of records, host his own prime-time television show, star in movies, and secure a position as one of the true superstars of country music.

Johnny Cash didn't struggle for very long before emerging as a wealthy and successful entertainer. Unlike some musicians, he didn't spend too many years working in rough-and-tumble bars where the risk to life and limb was sometimes greater than the pay. As legend goes in the music business, Johnny didn't pay as much dues as most people do before they make it to the top. However, there is more than one way to measure the hardships a person experiences. Too often fame and fortune can create more problems than they solve. For a long time, Johnny Cash's success was little more than a heavy cross to bear. But unlike so many other stars who let themselves get done in by the pitfalls of wealth and notoriety, Johnny managed to turn a potential tragedy into a story with a happy ending.

## Beginnings

Poverty is a relative term. A wealthy person might consider herself poor if her income dropped off from a million dollars one year to fifty thousand the next. A poor man who has little to eat might consider himself rich if he suddenly found the money for a steak dinner lying on the road. Americans love rags-to-riches stories, and that is the case with many of our country music stars.

Johnny Cash was born in 1932, the height of the Great Depression, in Kingsland, Arkansas. His family wasn't as poor as some. In his autobiography, *Man in Black,* Johnny reveals that his parents greatly resent being painted as poverty-stricken farmers.

"I don't believe a man ever lived who worked harder . . . to (provide) for his family than my father," Johnny recalls. "When the Depression hit in '29, my daddy was one of the few men in Cleveland County, Arkansas, who could usually find work of some kind. He cut pulpwood, worked at sawmills and on the railroad . . . which along with all the food and animals he raised not only fed us, but some of the more needy neighbors as well."

By 1935, economic conditions weren't getting much better. So when Ray Cash heard about the federal government's resettlement project in Dyess, Arkansas, he didn't hesitate to pick up his family and their few possessions and relocate. Because Ray Cash was so hard-working, he and his family were able to eke out a better living than most. Johnny has vivid memories of picking cotton alongside his father and five brothers and sisters. In time, the Cashes greatly improved themselves to the point that they eventually owned forty acres of farmland.

Like most other families in the area, the Cashes depended on music as their primary source of entertainment. In 1936, they purchased their first radio. On quiet evenings, they sat and listened to the Carter Family sing traditional hymns and southern folk music. The Carter's music was more than entertainment, though. As author Greil Marcus points out in his book, *Mystery Train,* this music was central to the lives of folk in the rural South:

> *The Carter Family . . . were the first to record the old songs everyone knew, to make the shared musical culture concrete, and their music drew a circle around the community. They celebrated the landscape, found strength in a feel for death because it was the only certainty, laughed a bit, and promised to leave the hillbilly home they helped build only on a gospel ship.*

But there were other forces at work on young men of Johnny Cash's age. There was a feeling that although their parents had done well in coping with a tough situation, it would, at some point, be necessary to leave the farm and try one's luck in the city. The outbreak of World War II made this feeling a reality. But even in the twenties, country music pioneer Jimmy Rodgers foresaw the kind of restlessness that was to cause Johnny Cash and many of his contemporaries to break loose from the rural community. Greil Marcus explains Rodgers's influence this way:

> *He was every boy who ever ran away from home, hanging out in the railroad yards, bumming around with black minstrels, pushing out the limits of his life . . . He bragged about gun-play on Beale Street, played jazz with Louis Armstrong, and though there was melancholy in his soul, his smile was a good one. He sounded like a man who could make a home for himself anywhere. There's so much* room *in this country, he seemed to be saying, so many things to do—how could an honest man be satisfied to live within the frontiers he was born to?*

Johnny Cash is a man who prides himself on sticking close to his roots. But there is little doubt that he had an inkling that he was cut out for something more extraordinary than a life of farming and chopping cotton. During his boyhood, he would gather around the radio with the rest of his family and take in the music of the Carters, Jimmy Rodgers, Hank Williams, Ernest Tubb, and others. Johnny's family was musical, especially on his mother's side, and there was always a lot of singing going on. But when Johnny's older brother Roy formed a band in the late thirties and managed to perform over a local radio station, something began to click for the youngster. Individual singing stars who wrote their own songs were becoming an important force in country music, and Johnny dreamed of carving out a niche for himself.

After he graduated from high school in 1950, Johnny moved to Detroit and took a job in the booming auto industry. One year later, he enlisted in the air force and became a radio intercept operator. During his years in the service, Johnny bought his first guitar. As a youngster in Arkansas, he had written a number of poems. Now he wrote frequently, always trying to set his poems to music. In 1954, Johnny left the service and decided to settle in Memphis. Shortly after that, he married his first wife, Vivian Liberto. Within a year the couple had their first child, Rosanne.

After trying unsuccessfully to make a living as a door-to-door salesman, Johnny was determined to become a full-time musician. Through his brother Roy, Johnny met two other aspiring young musicians—Marshall Grant and Luther Perkins—and formed a band. With Grant on string bass and Perkins on electric guitar, the three rehearsed Johnny's songs along with current country hits by Hank Snow and others. There was little evidence for anyone to predict Johnny's phenomenal success. Had it not been for that fateful meeting with Sam Phillips in 1955, Johnny Cash might have remained a good amateur or semi-professional singer. As it happened, he soon became one of America's most popular stars.

Between 1956–58, Johnny was America's top country artist. Some of his better-known hits on Sun included: "Ballad of a Teenage Queen," "Guess Things Happen That Way," and "The Ways of a Woman in Love." By 1958, Johnny had sold over six million records and moved to the much bigger Columbia Records. He had also cut out a place for himself as a songwriter, with versions of his tunes recorded by everyone from Hoagy Carmichael to Lawrence Welk. But many of Johnny's most memorable records were penned by other writers: "The Ballad of Ira Hayes," about an American Indian war hero who died a forgotten alcoholic, was written by Peter Lafarge; and "A Boy Named Sue," a song about proving one's manhood, was written by Shel Silverstein.

Success followed Johnny into the sixties, as he turned out a seemingly endless stream of hit records. By the end of the decade, he had won countless grammys and Country Music Association Awards. Although he has earned millions of dollars, Johnny always sympathized with the less fortunate. He was an outspoken supporter of American Indians. He recorded an album, *Bitter Tears*, which addressed itself to the plight of these forgotten Americans. He also played many benefits for Indian and other humanitarian causes.

Another of Johnny Cash's deep concerns has been

the cruel and dehumanizing effects of prison. Beginning with a New Year's Day concert at California's San Quentin Prison, Johnny went on to play and record albums at prisons in Arkansas, Texas, Kansas, and Tennessee. Johnny sums up his feelings about the loneliness of prison this way:

*You sit on your cold, steel mattressless bush and watch a cockroach crawl out from under the filthy commode, and you don't kill it. You envy the roach as you watch it crawl out under the cell door.*

Although Johnny Cash has never been convicted of a felony or served a jail term, he has spent some long and painful nights in the cells of various county prisons. But his understanding of the prisoner's plight comes not so much from these brief stints behind bars as much as from the spiritual and emotional prison that he lived in for years. Unable to cope with the pressures of wealth and success, Johnny became addicted to pills. As a result, he often became violent and self-destructive, and woke up in the hospital or in jail.

It's not difficult for musicians and performers to become hooked on pills. In fact, it takes a strong person to avoid the immediate fix that drugs offer. There are the long miles that even the most successful performers must log in traveling from one performance to the next. After traveling hundreds of miles and arriving in still another town for still another one-night stand, it's common to feel a bit tired and dragged out. To the performer, it all gets to be routine—he plays the same set, makes the same moves, and tells the same little jokes between songs as the night before. On the other hand, the audience has paid money and is all excited about this special evening. Performers feel obliged to return the excitement of their fans in kind. What, then, could be more natural than a little pick-me-up to raise one's tired spirits? This pick-me-up in pill form is known as amphetamines or speed. In his autobiography, *Man in Black,* Johnny refers to it as "a demon called Deception:"

> *With all the traveling I had to do . . . those pills could pep me up and make me feel like doing a show. I got a handful of the little white ones . . . (which were) just one of a variety of a dozen or more shapes and sizes. . . . They had a whole bunch of nice little names for them to dress them up, and they came in all colors. . . . Inside that bottle of . . . pills, which cost only eight or ten dollars for a hundred, came at no extra cost a demon called Deception.*

When Johnny first started taking the pills, he felt as if they were more of a help than a hindrance. Not only did they pick him up when he was tired, they also pushed away any fear or self-doubt he might have had before a performance. While he was taking pills on just an occasional basis, Johnny thought he was doing just fine. He goes on to say:

> With a couple of those pills in me . . . I had courage and confidence. . . . My timing was superb. My energy was multiplied. I enjoyed every song in every concert and could perform with a driving, relentless intensity. . . . If I'd ever been shy before an audience, I wasn't anymore. I rattled off my lines of dialogue between songs that kept people entertained. I was personable, outgoing, energetic—I loved everybody!

In time, though, Johnny became addicted to those pills. He realized that they were no longer just an occasional thing, but a serious problem that threatened to destroy him. Johnny's performances started to go downhill, as did his personal life. He became unreliable, dishonest, and violent as the pills brought out things in his personality that made his life "a living hell."

In recent years, the world has learned of many performers in pop and country music who had similar problems. But perhaps the biggest revelation involved Elvis Presley, the man who started his career in the same Memphis recording studio as Johnny.

"There are so many of us that started in the mid-fifties that are gone now," Johnny recently told Harry Reasoner of "Sixty Minutes." "There were people supplying me (with pills) who had written me off—some prominent people in the music business

**48**

who wanted me to go down with them. But my friends and loved ones kept them away. (In order to kick the pill habit) I locked myself in my room and climbed the walls for thirty days."

Johnny believes that one of the things that contributed to Elvis's demise was the people who were around him. Between the bodyguards, groupies, and other hangers-on, there were few loved ones to lean on when things got tough. As hard as it is for the public to believe, the life of a superstar can be much tougher than that of an average person. While it is true that most music business idols are rich and famous, it takes a strong person to handle the pressures that accompany stardom. Elvis, for instance, was such a big star so early in life that he had very little personal strength to fall back on when pressures started mounting. It was almost as though he believed the myths the fan magazines had created about him. When Johnny Cash reminisces about how he and Elvis started out together and how both of them became addicted to pills, he humbly says, "There but for the grace of God goes me."

## The Turnaround

Thinking about it now, Johnny Cash realizes that the big difference between him and casualties like Elvis is the support of a loving family. Although he is

Elvis Presley—plenty of groupies, but few loved
ones to lean on.

often pictured as a lonely man dressed in black, Johnny is surrounded by friends and loved ones. Most of the people in his band are close personal friends whom he calls "members of my musical family." But the closest and most important person in his life is his second wife, June Carter Cash.

As a member of the original Carter family, June is part of the folk tradition that is at the root of Johnny's music. But her musical support is only one reason why Johnny introduces her in his performances as, "the biggest hit in my life for the last twenty years." When they first met, Johnny was already a big star, and June was a regular on the Grand Ole Opry. She joined his tour while Johnny was in the depths of his pill problem. Because of her love for him, June dedicated herself to helping him overcome his addiction.

"I became a thief," she told Harry Reasoner. "I stole pills. I stole his car keys. I did everything I could and I did things I never would have done ordinarily. But I . . . didn't know what else to do. I thought he would die (so) I flushed . . . his amphetamines and barbiturates (down the toilet)."

Johnny credits June with turning his life around. Although he had turned out a remarkable string of hits during the sixties, he had also hit the lowest point in his life. But with June's love and a revitalized faith in Christianity, Johnny was able to start a new life.

In 1968, the couple married, and two years later they had their first son, John Carter Cash. Today John Carter accompanies his parents on the road when schoolwork permits. As much as possible, the Cash family tries to keep their real family bonds and musical connections one and the same. At various times, the troupe has featured June's sisters, Anita and Helen, her daughter (from a previous marriage) Carlene, Johnny's daughter Rosanne, Mother Maybelle Carter, and various other family members. It would be fair to say that Johnny Cash's personal turnaround came as a result of replacing pills with religious convictions and strong family values.

## Let's not Forget the Music

When Johnny gave up drugs and married June, a friend half-jokingly asked him, "Who are they going to gossip about in Nashville now?"

"They'll find someone," John replied.

Go into your local magazine store and you'll find that the headlines are usually talking about who's cheating on whom and who's taking what drugs. For years, Johnny Cash was such a good topic for gossip that people tended to forget how important he was to country music. Yet in spite of his personal problems,

Johnny achieved a national recognition by the end of the sixties that was unmatched in country music history.

Never one to abide by musical formulas, Johnny recorded albums of hymns and traditional folk material (*Ride This Train*), albums about the toils and troubles of the working man (*Blood, Sweat and Tears*), and albums about the plight of American Indians (*Bitter Tears*). He has also recorded songs by younger songwriters like Bob Dylan and Kris Kristofferson. His live shows are mixtures of all these musical influences. But whether he is singing live or on record, hymn or contemporary pop song, the sound is unmistakably and uniquely Johnny Cash.

Johnny's combination of musical tradition and innovation is, perhaps, his most outstanding contribution. He is—through his own efforts and his association with the Carter family—a permanent part of the American folk and country tradition. His desire and ability to experiment with any kind of contemporary material that appeals to him also makes him an innovative force to be reckoned with in contemporary country music. Recent solo efforts by John's daughter Rosanne and June's daughter Carlene also point to the continuation of the Cash-Carter influence for many years to come.

# Good Works

We may hate to admit it, but some of our favorite media personalities just aren't very nice human beings. In many cases, they are selfish individuals with no sense of social responsibility and no desire to give something back to the people who make their success possible. One of the things that makes a popular performer a genuine superstar is the very real desire to do something positive to improve the human condition.

Even in those years when Johnny Cash was having intense personal problems, he was vitally concerned with helping less fortunate people. His work on behalf of American Indians and prisoners is only the beginning. This man who earns some five million dollars a year has always identified with the poor, the down and out, the unfortunate people of this world. On his network television show, which ran for three years in the early seventies, in his many benefit appearances and in his anonymous, charitable contributions, Johnny Cash has tried to share his values and convictions with the rest of the world.

Although he has shied away from politics, Johnny has always spoken freely about his beliefs. During the Vietnam War years, he took the unpopular stance of supporting the military draft and the war because that is what he believed. These days, Johnny speaks a great deal about his religious beliefs. He often appears with evangelist Billy Graham and has often been quoted as saying: "I don't have a career anymore. What I have now is a ministry."

What's ahead for Johnny Cash? He has already achieved everything one can in the field of country music. He has won every award, been selected to the Country Music Hall of Fame, contributed to all kinds of worthy causes, written an autobiography, hosted countless television specials, acted in a number of fine films, and even produced a film (on the life of Christ). With so much under his belt, you might think that Johnny would want to sit back and relax. Nothing could be further from his mind. He still pursues a heavy recording and performing schedule, takes an active role in looking after his extensive business interests—which include banking, real estate, and trucking—and involves himself in whatever other projects he deems worthy of his time.

Johnny Cash isn't thinking about slowing down. He plans to be a major force in shaping the direction that country music will take in the years to come. "I'm fifty years old," he told Harry Reasoner, "(but) I feel like my life has just begun."

# Johnny Cash Collector's Guide

| YEAR | ALBUM | LABEL |
|------|-------|-------|
| 1958 | The Fabulous Johnny Cash | Columbia |
| 1963 | Blood Sweat and Tears | Columbia |
| 1963 | Ring of Fire | Columbia |
| 1964 | I Walk the Line | Columbia |
| 1964 | Bitter Tears/Ballads of the American Indian | Columbia |
| 1965 | Orange Blossom Special | Columbia |
| 1966 | Everybody Loves a Nut | Columbia |
| 1967 | Greatest Hits Volume I | Columbia |
| 1967 | Carrying On with June Carter | Columbia |
| 1968 | From Sea to Shining Sea | Columbia |
| 1968 | At Folsom Prison | Columbia |
| 1969 | Holy Land | Columbia |
| 1969 | Johnny Cash | Harmony |
| 1969 | Original Golden Hits Volume I and II | Sun |
| 1970 | Show Time with Tennessee Two | Sun |
| 1970 | Story Songs of Trains and Rivers with Tennessee Two | Sun |
| 1970 | Hello I'm Johnny Cash | Columbia |
| 1970 | The World of Johnny Cash | Columbia |
| 1970 | Singing Storyteller with Tennessee Two | Sun |
| 1970 | Jackson (with June Carter) | Columbia |
| 1970 | Living Legend | Sun |
| 1970 | Get Rhythm | Sun |
| 1970 | The Johnny Cash Show | Epic |
| 1970 | Rough Cut King of Country Music | Sun |
| 1970 | Sunday Down South with Jerry Lee Lewis | Sun |
| 1971 | Show | Columbia |

| YEAR | ALBUM | LABEL |
|------|-------|-------|
| 1971 | Man, the World, his Music | Sun |
| 1971 | Man in Black | Columbia |
| 1971 | Sings Hank Williams (with Jerry Lee Lewis) | Sun |
| 1971 | Collections-Great Hits Volume II | Columbia |
| 1972 | Original Golden Hits Volume III | Sun |
| 1972 | A Thing Called Love | Columbia |
| 1972 | Folsom Prison Blues | Columbia |
| 1972 | Give My Love to Rose (with June Carter) | Harmony |
| 1972 | America | Columbia |
| 1972 | Johnny Cash Songbook | Harmony |
| 1973 | Any Old Wind That Blows | Columbia |
| 1973 | I Walk the Line | Nash |
| 1973 | Johnny Cash and his Woman (with June Carter) | Columbia |
| 1974 | At San Quentin | Columbia |
| 1974 | Ragged Old Flag | Columbia |
| 1975 | Johnny Cash Sings Precious Memories | Columbia |
| 1975 | John R. Cash | Columbia |
| 1976 | Strawberry Cake | Columbia |
| 1976 | One Piece at a Time | Columbia |
| 1977 | Last Gunfighter Ballad | Columbia |
| 1977 | The Rambler | Columbia |
| 1978 | I Would Like to See You Again | Columbia |
| 1979 | Johnny Cash's Greatest Hits Volume III | Columbia |
| 1979 | Silver | Columbia |
| 1980 | A Believer Sings the Truth | Columbia |
| 1980 | Rockabilly Blues | Columbia |
| 1981 | The Baron | Columbia |
| 1982 | The Survivors (with Jerry Lee Lewis and Carl Perkins) | Columbia |

| YEAR | SINGLE | LABEL | C&W | POP |
|------|--------|-------|-----|-----|
| 1955 | Cry, Cry, Cry | Sun | | |
| 1956 | Folsom Prison Blues/So Doggone Lonesome | Sun | * | |
| 1956 | I Walk the Line | Sun | * | x |
| 1956 | There You Go/Train of Love | Sun | * | |
| 1957 | Next in Line/Don't Make Me Go | Sun | * | x |
| 1957 | Home of the Blues/Give My Love to Rose | Sun | * | x |
| 1958 | Ballad of a Teenage Queen | Sun | * | x |
| 1958 | Big River | Sun | | x |
| 1958 | Guess Things Happen That Way/Come in Stranger | Sun | * | x |
| 1958 | The Ways of a Woman in Love/You're the Nearest Thing to Heaven | Sun | * | x |
| 1958 | I Just Thought You'd Like to Know | Sun | | x |
| 1958 | What Do I Care | Columbia | * | x |
| 1958 | All Over Again | Columbia | * | x |
| 1959 | It's Just About Time | Sun | | x |
| 1959 | Don't Take Your Guns to Town | Columbia | * | x |
| 1959 | Luther Played the Boogie | Sun | * | |
| 1959 | Thanks a Lot | Sun | | |
| 1959 | Frankie's Man Johnny | Columbia | * | x |
| 1959 | You Dreamer You | Columbia | | |
| 1959 | Katy Too | Sun | | x |
| 1959 | I Got Stripes | Columbia | * | x |
| 1959 | Five Feet High and Rising | Columbia | | x |
| 1959 | Goodbye Little Darling | Sun | | |
| 1960 | Little Drummer Boy | Columbia | | x |
| 1960 | Straight A's in Love | Sun | | x |
| 1960 | I Love You Because | Sun | | |
| 1960 | Seasons Of My Heart | Columbia | * | |

**58**

| YEAR | SINGLE | LABEL | C&W | POP |
|------|--------|-------|-----|-----|
| 1960 | Smiling Bill McCall | Columbia | | |
| 1960 | Down the Street to 301 | Sun | | x |
| 1960 | Honky-Tonk Girl | Columbia | | x |
| 1960 | Second Honeymoon | Columbia | | x |
| 1961 | Oh Lonesome Me | Sun | | x |
| 1961 | Mean-Eyed Cat | Sun | | |
| 1961 | The Rebel Johnny Yuma | Columbia | | |
| 1961 | Tennessee Flat-Top Boy | Columbia | | x |
| 1962 | Big Battle | Columbia | | |
| 1962 | In the Jailhouse Now | Columbia | * | |
| 1962 | Bonozo | Sun | | x |
| 1963 | Busted | Columbia | | |
| 1963 | Ring of Fire | Columbia | * | x |
| 1963 | The Matador | Columbia | * | x |
| 1964 | Understand Your Man | Columbia | * | x |
| 1964 | Dark as a Dungeon | Columbia | | |
| 1964 | The Ballad of Ira Hayes | Columbia | * | |
| 1964 | Bad News | Columbia | * | |
| 1964 | It Ain't Me Babe | Columbia | * | x |
| 1965 | Orange Blossom Special | Columbia | * | x |
| 1965 | Master Garfield | Columbia | | |
| 1965 | The Sons of Katie Elder | Columbia | * | |
| 1965 | Happy To Be with You | Columbia | * | |
| 1966 | The One On the Right Is On the Left | Columbia | * | x |
| 1966 | Everybody Loves a Nut | Columbia | | x |
| 1966 | Boa Constrictor | Columbia | | |
| 1966 | You Beat All I Ever Saw | Columbia | | |
| 1967 | Jackson with June Carter | Columbia | * | |
| 1967 | Long-Legged Guitar-Pickin' Man | Columbia | * | |
| 1967 | Rosanna's Going Wild | Columbia | * | x |
| 1968 | Folsom Prison Blues | Columbia | * | x |
| 1968 | Daddy Sang Bass | Columbia | * | x |

* Smash Hit
X Crossover to Pop

**59**

| YEAR | SINGLE | LABEL | C&W | POP |
|---|---|---|---|---|
| 1969 | A Boy Named Sue | Columbia | * | x |
| 1969 | Get Rhythm | Sun | | x |
| 1969 | Blistered/See Ruby Fall | Columbia | * | x |
| 1970 | If I Were a Carpenter (with June Carter) | Columbia | * | x |
| 1970 | What Is Truth | Columbia | * | x |
| 1970 | Sunday Morning Coming Down | Columbia | * | x |
| 1970 | Flesh Blood | Columbia | * | x |
| 1970 | Rock Island Line | Sun | * | x |
| 1971 | Man in Black | Columbia | * | x |
| 1971 | Singing in Vietnam Talking Blues | Columbia | | |
| 1971 | No Need To Work (with June Carter) | Columbia | | |
| 1971 | Papa Was a Good Man | Columbia | | |
| 1972 | A Thing Called Love | Columbia | * | |
| 1972 | Kate | Columbia | * | x |
| 1972 | If I Had a Hammer (with June Carter) | Columbia | | |
| 1972 | Oney | Columbia | * | |
| 1972 | The World Needs a Melody (with the Carter Family) | Columbia | | |
| 1972 | Any Old Wind That Blows | Columbia | * | |
| 1973 | The Loving Gift (with June Carter) | Columbia | | |
| 1973 | Children | Columbia | | |
| 1973 | Praise the Lord and Pass the Soup (with the Carter Family) | Columbia | | |
| 1973 | Allegheny (with June Carter) | Columbia | | |
| 1973 | Pick the Wildwood Flower (with Mother Maybelle and the Carter Family) | Columbia | | |
| 1974 | Orleans Parish Prison | Columbia | | |
| 1974 | Ragged Old Flag | Columbia | | |
| 1974 | Lady Came From Baltimore | Columbia | | |
| 1975 | My Old Kentucky Home (Turpentine and Dandelion Wine) | Columbia | | |
| 1975 | Look at Them Beans | Columbia | | |

| YEAR | SINGLE | LABEL | C&W | POP |
|------|--------|-------|-----|-----|
| 1975 | Texas 1947 | Columbia | | |
| 1976 | Strawberry Cake | Columbia | | |
| 1976 | One Piece at a Time | Columbia | * | x |
| 1976 | Sold Out of Flagpoles | Columbia | | |
| 1976 | It's All Over | Columbia | | |
| 1976 | Old Time Feeling (with June Carter Cash) | Columbia | | |
| 1977 | The Last Gunfighter's Ballad | Columbia | | |
| 1977 | Lady | Columbia | | |
| 1977 | After the Ball | Columbia | | |
| 1978 | I Would Like To See You Again | Columbia | | |
| 1978 | It'll Be Her | Columbia | | |
| 1978 | There Ain't No Good Chain Gang (with Waylon Jennings) | Columbia | * | |
| 1979 | I Will Rock and Roll with You | Columbia | | |
| 1979 | (Ghost) Riders in the Sky | Columbia | * | |
| 1979 | I'll Say It's True/Cocaine Blues | Columbia | | |
| 1979 | I Wish I Was Crazy Again (with Waylon Jennings) | Columbia | | |
| 1980 | Bull Rider | Columbia | | |
| 1980 | Song of the Patriot (harmony vocals with Marty Robbins) | Columbia | | |
| 1980 | Cold Lonesome Morning | Columbia | | |
| 1980 | The Last Time | Columbia | | |
| 1981 | Without Love | Columbia | | |
| 1981 | Mobile Boy | Columbia | | |
| 1981 | Chattanooga City Limits/Reverend Mr. Black | Columbia | | |
| 1982 | The General Lee | Epic | | |
| 1982 | Georgia on a Fast Train | Columbia | | |
| 1983 | We Must Believe in Magic | Columbia | | |
| 1983 | I'm Ragget Right | Columbia | | |

* Smash Hit
X Crossover to Pop

Loretta Lynn—"coal miner's daughter."

*I was pushed into the music business. . . . I didn't really want to
get into it; (My husband) was the one who wanted me to do it.*
                                    *Loretta Lynn,* Rolling Stone

How do you become a country music superstar?
The first step is almost always to have a dream and a
burning desire to get to the top. But unlike most of
the other people in this book, Loretta Lynn never
thought much about making it in the entertainment
business. Nevertheless, she is one of the most successful performers in the history of country music.

By her own admission, that success would never
have come about without her husband's planning and
pushing. Even today, it is Mr. Lynn who oversees
Loretta's career and calls most of the shots. But
Loretta is no puppet with someone else pulling the
strings. Far from it. In a music scene that is often
associated with a conservative point of view and old-
fashioned values, Loretta Lynn has emerged as the
most outspoken, controversial woman in country
music. Although she is not an official supporter of the
woman's liberation movement, Loretta is one of
America's most visible spokespersons on the issue of
equal rights for women. Here is a sampling of some
of her more choice remarks over the years:

*'Men can't get their egos hurt. They think it's okay for them to
do what they do but bad for a woman. . . . What's good for the
gander is good for the goose.'* (Newsweek)

*'I almost got an all-girl band . . . But people started saying, "If you had one incident, people would start gossiping about it." It was the old double standard again.'* (Village Voice)

*I think it's good for people to realize that women can do things as good as a man. And I think show business is one of the places where that's true. There's more women stars in Nashville all the time . . . and they're proving they can do the job the same as a man.* (Rolling Stone)

These are almost revolutionary statements for a woman of Loretta's background. The words to the first verse of a song called "Waggoner's Lad" offer a more traditional point of view for someone born and bred in the rural South of the 1930s:

*Oh hard is the fortune*
*of all woman kind,*
*She's always controlled,*
*she's always confined,*
*Controlled by her parents*
*until she's a wife,*
*A slave to her husband*
*for the rest of her life.*
                    *("Waggoner's Lad")*

The words to this Appalachian folksong could have served as an apt description of how Loretta Lynn's life might have turned out had it not been for a few unusual twists of fate. She was, after all, a poor Kentucky coal miner's daughter who grew up in Butcher Hollow, a place that Loretta herself admits might be "the most backward part of the United States." Although she grew up in a one-room shack without running water and only attended school through the eighth grade, Loretta has no regrets about her humble beginnings.

"Being poor really helped me," she says in her autobiography—*Coal Miner's Daughter*. "In some ways, that was the best part of my life, learning how to survive."

In spite of her fond memories, however, growing up in Butcher "Holler" (that's how the folks who live there pronounce it) during the Depression was not easy. There were times when Melvin Webb (Loretta's daddy) could not bring in enough money to feed and clothe his family. He had worked in the lumber mills until the Depression, but when hard times caused them to close, Melvin Webb found himself out of work. After the Depression eased up, there were some jobs in the coal mines. Although he had never been a miner before, Loretta's daddy could not pass up this chance to provide for his family. "I felt real proud of daddy for working in the mines," Loretta affectionately recalls in her autobiography. "It must have taken a lot of nerve to go into that terrible dark hole. . . . He kept his family alive by breaking his own body down. That's the only way to look at it."

The Butcher Holler days are long behind Loretta now. She is working on her third decade as one of country music's brightest superstars. Her face has been on the cover of national magazines, and her best-selling autobiography has been turned into an award-winning film. Yet in many respects, Loretta Lynn seems as unimpressed by her success as her friends and relatives back in the hills of Kentucky.

"My folks don't make a big fuss over me," she confesses in *Coal Miner's Daughter.* "They knew me when I was wearing flour sacks, so I ain't no big deal to them. I can go back there and we'll talk the same as we always did."

Loretta recognizes that one of the things that makes her so appealing to country music fans is the humble beginnings she shares with many of them. And while she is fiercely proud of her background, she understands how far she has come:

"I wouldn't take nothing for the memories of what I went through—but I don't want to go back to it. I remember being hungry too much. I think maybe it's worse today because people know they're poor from watching TV news and stuff. Back then we didn't know we were poor, and people were proud."

Loretta's humble beginnings are not very different from those of most other country stars. But unlike many of them, she never dreamed of making it big in the music business. There was always music in the Webb household. Her grandfather played the banjo while the rest of the clan gathered round and sang. There was a lot of talent in Loretta's family. One of her sisters is Crystal Gayle—now a big star in her own right—and another, Peggy Sue, wrote some of Loretta's hits and recorded under her own name.

Up until the time she was thirteen, Loretta's life was just what you might expect from a young girl growing up in that time and place. She went to school, pitched in with the chores, and played with the other kids. But when she was in the eighth grade, Loretta met nineteen-year-old Oliver Vanetta Lynn—the man who was to become her husband and the most important person in her life. In *Coal Miner's Daughter*, Loretta tells the famous story of how she met the man she calls Doolittle or Doo. There was a pie-bidding contest at the local schoolhouse in which the man who bid the most money for a pie got to take home the girl who baked it. Loretta wasn't much of a cook, but her husband-to-be was determined to win her pie, and her favor. Doolittle started bidding against another boy named Flop Murphy. They started with fifty cents and kept topping each other until they got up to $4.50. Suddenly, Doolittle shouted out, "Five dollars and sold." He had won the pie and the privilege of taking its baker home.

When the contest was over, Doolittle decided to try a piece of Loretta's pie. Unfortunately, he had no idea that she accidentally used salt instead of sugar in preparing it. He took one bite and tried very hard not to gag. But in spite of his salty surprise, Doolittle was extremely attracted to Loretta.

Later that night, Doolittle drove Loretta home in his jeep, promising that he would see her soon. Her folks were not too pleased about Loretta going with a man who was so much older, and with a bad reputation to boot. But the next night, he pulled up to her house in his jeep. The two dated for a few months, after which Doolittle asked Loretta to marry him. While her parents felt Loretta was not ready for marriage, they probably realized that there was little they could do to prevent it.

"They didn't exactly say yes," Loretta recalls. "But I knew we were going to do it. After Doo went home, Mommy and Daddy cried all night and didn't hardly talk to me. . . . Daddy made Doo promise not to whip me, and not to take me too far from home. And Mommy told me, 'This is something you'll regret for the rest of your life.'"

The marriage had its problems from the start. Doolittle had served in the Army during World War II and was a man of the world. Loretta, on the other hand, was an innocent thirteen-year-old who had never been more than a few miles from home. After some rough going at the beginning and a temporary separation, the young couple reunited. Some time later, Loretta gave birth to their first child.

Loretta admits that marriage at thirteen and motherhood at fourteen are not the smartest things a young girl can do. Since she took this road herself, who could possibly be more qualified to criticize it? That's a big part of Loretta's appeal: the way she brings her real life feelings into everything she says and sings. Country performers often take pride in their honesty. But Loretta is more than just honest. She is downright blunt.

Loretta was far too young to put up very much resistance against anything Doolittle decided to do during those first few years. Typically, a young man in Butcher Holler goes to work in the mines while his wife starts having babies. The couple was well under way with the baby part, but Doolittle had no intention of becoming a miner. Although it meant breaking one of the promises he had made to Loretta's daddy, Doolittle moved his family thousands of miles away to the state of Washington. There were opportunities in the timber business there, and Doo wasn't about to pass up a chance to make a better life for his growing family, even if it did mean taking Loretta far away from Butcher Holler.

For their first few years in Washington, Loretta cooked and cleaned at the ranch where they lived with other people. Meanwhile, Doolittle worked hard, often holding down two jobs. The couple was certainly living much better than their families and friends in Butcher Holler, but Doo was far from satisfied. He had often heard Loretta singing around the house, and he believed she sounded every bit as good as the singers who were on he radio. In his mind's eye, Doo already pictured Loretta as the next big country music star.

Loretta had no aspirations to get into the music business. By the time she was eighteen, she had four children, and being a wife and mother took up most of her time and energy. But Doolittle had his vision and nothing was going to stop him. He bought Loretta a guitar and encouraged her to practice regularly. He also started going around to local clubs, talking to musicians about his talented wife.

Band members who work in clubs are used to dealing with husbands who believe their wives have the makings of stars. Ambitious, outgoing guys like Doolittle are always bugging musicians to let this one or that one sit in. More often than not, the would-be star has very little talent.

The Penn Brothers were a local club band with their own radio show in Washington. Doolittle had been nagging them for weeks to let Loretta sit in with them. Finally they consented to let her audition at their house.

No one was more surprised than Loretta when the Penn Brothers showed up the morning after the audition to offer her a job with their band. They also said they wanted to tape her performance and air it on their radio show. "I got scared, real scared," Loretta admits in her autobiography. "Doolittle told me I was going to sing, scared or not. He told me I was stupid. That made me so mad I made up my mind to sing."

It was 1961, almost ten years since Loretta and Doolittle had left Butcher Holler. Her music career had just gotten under way, but things were moving fast. A few months after that first nervous audition with the Penn Brothers, Loretta started her own band, Loretta's Trail Blazers. She was now working six nights a week in halls and clubs around Custer, Washington, and gaining a good deal of local popularity.

Loretta's first real break came when she appeared on a Tacoma, Washington, television show hosted by Buck Owens. The show was an amateur contest which Loretta won easily. It was on this show that Norman Burleigh, owner of a small Canadian label called Zero Records, first heard Loretta sing. Burleigh, who made his fortune in the lumber business, arranged for Loretta to go to Los Angeles to record one of her own songs, "I'm a Honky-Tonk Girl." The record sounded like a hit, but neither Burleigh nor the Lynns had any idea of how to promote it properly.

As usual, Doolittle wasn't about to let anything stop him from realizing his ambitions. He had 3,500 copies of a home photograph of Loretta printed up, and he mailed it and the record to every country station whose address he could find.

The record began receiving radio play and soon made the country music top twenty. But there was very little distribution set up. This meant that if people heard "I'm a Honky-Tonk Girl" on the radio and wanted to buy the record, they usually were unable to find it at their local record store. Doolittle tried to solve this problem by supplying the record stores himself, while still holding down a full-time job as a car mechanic.

Norman Burleigh decided that the only way to launch Loretta's career was to send her to Nashville. Backed by his money, Loretta and Doolittle left the children with their parents and took off for the capital of country music in a '55 Ford. They slept in the back of the car and lived on bologna and cheese sandwiches. On the way to Nashville, the Lynns stopped off at twenty to thirty radio stations a day asking the DJ's to plug their song. When they got to a radio station, Loretta would put on her one presentable dress, walk in, and introduce herself. Sometimes the disc jockeys would play the record and even interview her over the air. Doolittle would wait outside in the car, ready to hit the next radio station on the way to Nashville. Loretta recalls the surprise of one disc jockey when she told him the Lynns were distributing and promoting the record themselves. Trying to be helpful, he reminded her that it usually takes at least three or four years to get on the Grand Ole Opry and become a big star. "Maybe so," Loretta recalls telling him in *Coal Miner's Daughter*, "but I can't wait that long." As it turned out, she didn't have to.

After Loretta and Doolittle arrived in Nashville at the end of their long and tiring trip, they dropped in on the Wilburn Brothers to play their record. Doyle and Teddy Wilburn were country music stars trying to get their own talent agency off the ground. At the time, the Wilburns weren't sure if they wanted to sign Loretta, because they felt she sounded a little too much like Kitty Wells, who was the then reigning queen of country music. After they finally decided to represent Loretta, the Wilburns signed her up with Decca Records and producer Owen Bradley. In 1962, she recorded her first number-one hit, "Success," a song that had the classic line that Loretta would often refer to in later interviews: "Success has made a failure of our home."

Whatever problems success would lead to in the coming years, it certainly brought Loretta money, fame, and a career that was to see her become the most influential female country music performer of her generation. If the dream of stardom had been only Doolittle's at the beginning, Loretta was now ready to jump in with both feet. After she received national exposure on the Wilburn Brothers television show, Loretta became a force to be reckoned with in country music.

The beginning of a string of hit singles and albums that continues for Loretta to this day started in 1962. It was also the beginning of numerous awards that she has won over the years, including: the Country Music Association's Top Female Artist, a Grammy, and CMA's Entertainer of the Year. This last award probably meant the most to Loretta since she was the first woman to win it.

If Loretta had someone to model herself after, it was Kitty Wells, who was a star while Loretta was still a young girl. In 1952, Kitty recorded a song called, "It Wasn't God Who Made Honky-Tonk Angels." The song was an answer to a Hank Thompson song entitled, "Wild Side Of Life." Thompson's song dealt with women who had gone wrong, a common topic of many country tunes. Kitty Wells's song put the blame for many of women's problems squarely on the shoulders of men. This point of view might not seem very extreme today, but it was quite shocking for that time and place. "It Wasn't God Who Made Honky-Tonk Angels" wasn't the first song to question the role of women in the rural South. But it was the first song with that point of view to become a number-one hit single. The idea that men should share the blame for some of the problems women had was revolutionary in a culture that portrayed women either as helpless victims or "honky-tonk angels." Here was an idea that Loretta could relate to both as a person and

Loretta with her sister, Crystal Gayle.

a personality looking to appeal to the younger generation of country listeners.

Loretta's timing appears to have been just right. Kitty Wells was still having hits, but she was past forty, and some of the younger fans found her a bit old-fashioned. Patsy Cline seemed a likely candidate to assume Kitty's throne, but her career was tragically cut short when she died in a plane crash in 1963. Loretta was a close friend of Patsy's, and she credited Patsy with being supportive and helpful. With the death of Patsy Cline and the aging of Kitty Wells, Loretta must have sensed that the field was now wide open for her.

Although there are definite traces of both Kitty and Patsy in Loretta's singing, it is probably more significant that Loretta followed their lead in establishing herself as a solo artist and band leader. Traditionally, women singers in the country field were part of real or fabricated "familes," or package shows. But Loretta sensed that her strongest identity lay in her individuality. She seemed to understand how to straddle the line between traditional country values and changing times.

"(Loretta) has modified her 'authenticity' with popular arrangements," observes Dorothy Horstman in *The Stars of Country Music*. In the same way, she manages to balance traditional rural southern values with what Horstman calls, "the sassy, spunky notion of women's 'territory.'" This has helped develop an audience for her music that includes everyone from "good old boys" to feminists. This is an image, Horstman believes, that is no accident, but a brilliant piece of marketing strategy. The proof of this is not only in the number of records Loretta sells, but also in different kinds of people who buy them.

Some of her songs like "Don't Come Home A Drinkin' (With Lovin' on Your Mind)" and "Your Squaw is on the Warpath" are highly appealing to female country music fans since they are direct warnings to men to keep their behavior under control. In "You Ain't Woman Enough (To Take My Man)," Loretta goes one step further when she tells a rival for her man, "I know where I stand, and you ain't woman enough to take my man." And in "Fist City," she goes so far as to say: "You better lay off my man . . . or I'll grab you by the hair of your head and lift you off the ground."

This was pretty strong stuff for a female country singer in the early sixties, and it won Loretta a fanatical following among women in the rural South. But in songs like "Coal Miner's Daughter," Loretta also hit a chord in city-dwelling women and men. They found her description of the simple virtues of rural life highly appealing. As Dorothy Horstman puts it:

> Loretta is an "original." Her appearance and voice conjure up pictures of smoky mountains, quaint cabins, pastoral lanes, a

*general store, and home folks rocking on the porch. To hillbilly and urban (listeners) alike, she's "authentic."*

Like most country music superstars, Loretta is highly sensitive to the feelings of her fans. She understands that country music fans are unusually devoted to the singers they adopt as their own. They play a very important role in a star's success, buying every record as soon as it comes out, calling radio stations requesting those records be played, and showing up at every performance they can get to. Loretta has become close friends with some of her earliest and most devoted fans. She openly credits them with much of her good fortune.

"When I look out over the crowd and see the same faces year after year," she told *Rolling Stone*, "I think I owe 'em more than just sayin' hello . . . I owe 'em everything I've got to give."

In order to keep herself prominent in her fans' hearts and minds, Loretta has to stay on the road a good part of the year. It is this kind of personal contact and high visibility that has made her and Doolittle wealthy enough to own their own town near Nashville, the nation's largest rodeo, several music publishing companies, and a talent agency (together with country singer Conway Twitty). So great is Loretta's national appeal that her autobiography, *Coal Miner's Daughter*, has been turned into an award-winning film. Still, she has had her problems over the years.

Unlike Willie Nelson and others who profess to love being "on the road again," Loretta is painfully aware that her life as a star has deprived her of the joys of having a real home life. "Money can buy you anything in the world," she told the *New York Post*, "but how can you be happy when you're never home? You can't be happy goin' from one town to another with the band every night, doin' a show, then goin' to the next town and cleanin' yourself up, maybe spendin' the night. This is not what I call happiness."

In addition to the pain of being far from her home and children so much of the time, Loretta has suffered her share of illnesses. She has been in the hospital several times over the years with a variety of ailments, some real and some fabricated by the press. Loretta has also been the target of several death threats. Understandably, these upset her very much. But she came to realize that the same qualities that make her so appealing to most people can sometimes touch off twisted emotions in a sick mind. Although she is not comfortable traveling with an armed bodyguard, she is convinced that it is necessary for her protection.

At one point, the death threats and health problems created so much publicity, they became the focal point of a major motion picture, Robert Altman's

*Nashville*. Although they weren't named in the film, it was clear that two of the main characters were based on Loretta and Doolittle. The film included scenes of the Loretta character fainting on stage and being shot at by a fan. Although she has passed out on stage a few times, Loretta denies any connection with the *Nashville* character. "If you're wondering whether that character . . . is me," she flatly states in her autobiography, "it ain't. . . . I've got my own life to lead."

Physical and emotional problems aside, Loretta has been leading a grand life. She still spends most of the year touring but she vacations a few months every winter at an ocean retreat in Mexico that she and Doolittle built. Admittedly, she still has some problems with her husband. But Loretta realizes that in the complex and fast-changing world we live in, there are no simple answers to the problems between men and women. Perhaps that is a key to understanding her enormous popularity.

Loretta's relationship with Doolittle may not be exemplary, yet she is a strong advocate of women's rights.

"I've always felt that a woman should be treated right," she told the *Village Voice*. Loretta understands, however, that it is not always easy for women to demand equality in day-to-day situations. "Sometimes (a woman) can't just walk up to somebody and say what she would like to," Loretta explained. "So if she can sing about it, it kind of helps her get it out of her system."

Loretta has been singing and talking about the things that are on her mind for many years now. Her song, "The Pill," has probably attracted more national attention from the media than any country song in history. Although she deeply loves her six children, she regrets having the first four at such an early age. The message of "The Pill" for other young women is the following: Think before you allow yourself to become pregnant, lest you become too tied down to get what you want out of life. Some radio stations objected to the song's message and refused to play it. Loretta's response in a *Newsweek* cover story was this: "If DJ's were women, there would be no confusion. The song's not dirty, it's threatening."

These are strong words from a simple country gal! The kind of words that get country singers on the covers of national magazines. Yet when Loretta says them, they come across sincerely. "I always said I'd never try to . . . beat around the bush just to keep from sayin' it just like it was," she told the *Village Voice*. "I like to say it just like it is."

What lies ahead for Loretta Lynn now that she has achieved so much more than she ever dreamed possible? In recent interviews, she has expressed a strong desire to spend more time out of the public eye. But this is not always as easy to do as it sounds. Popular superstars often have two opposing forces pulling at them. On the one hand, they make enough money to live in luxury for the rest of their lives. In theory, there is no financial need to keep working after a certain number of years if one handles the money carefully. But there are other considerations. A performer who stays out of the public eye for a couple of years has no guarantee that her fans won't feel deserted and turn their attentions elsewhere. You also don't get to be a superstar without taking a great deal of responsibility upon yourself. Loretta has a band and a large staff that she keeps on a year-round salary, whether she works or not. She also has various other buisness interests that feed off her popularity as a performer. But there comes a time when personal and emotional considerations outweigh all others. Loretta has indicated that she is well past that point. Here's what she says about her lack of a private life in *Coal Miner's Daughter*:

> *It's getting so bad, I don't even feel comfortable in my own house anymore. I get home for a day or two and by the time I unpack my bags and see what's changed since I left, it's time to get moving again. Then all my family and fans come to visit. . . . I start getting so nervous in my own house I sometimes even check into a motel in Nashville.*

After the book was turned into a movie, Loretta was asked if this added publicity wouldn't make her life even less private than it already was. "If you're going to let half the world know (all about your life), you might as well let the other half know too," she told the *New York Times*. In that same interview, however, Loretta also indicated a determination to move out of the public spotlight:

> *I've opened enough of my life like a book and now I'll quietly close some of it off. It's time for me and my husband to be by ourselves some more. . . . I guess the movie kind of finished what I started—or he started—a long time ago.*

How distant Loretta will be able to keep herself from the demands of her amazing career remains to be seen. But even if she never makes another record or gives another performance—and this is highly unlikely—her position as the most important female country star of her generation is secure. Here's how country music historian and radio personality Dorothy Horstman puts it:

> *Loretta is a transitional figure. Her career and her songs reflect the conflicts of a changing South perhaps better than any currently popular female country singer. As urbanization and sophistication continue their progress, the new voices that arise will be more liberated, more straightforward (and) more aggressive. . . . Where country music will end . . . is anybody's guess. But Loretta Lynn will continue to be a strong force for a good long time in "keeping it country."*

# Loretta Lynn Collector's Guide

| YEAR | ALBUM | LABEL |
|------|-------|-------|
| 1963 | Loretta Lynn Sings | Decca |
| 1964 | Before I'm Over You | Decca |
| 1965 | Songs From My Heart | Decca |
| 1965 | Blue Kentucky Girl | Decca, reissued MCA |
| 1965 | Ernest Tubb and Loretta Lynn | Decca |
| 1965 | Hyms | Decca, reissued MCA |
| 1966 | I Like 'Em Country | Decca |
| 1966 | You Ain't Woman Enough | Decca, reissued MCA |
| 1966 | Country Christmas | Decca, reissued MCA |
| 1967 | Don't Come Home A Drinkin' | Decca, reissued MCA |
| 1967 | Ernest Tubb and Loretta Lynn Singin' Again | Decca |
| 1967 | Singin' With Feeling | Decca |
| 1968 | Who Says God Is Dead | Decca, reissued MCA |
| 1968 | Here's Loretta Lynn | Vocalion, reissued Coral |
| 1968 | Fist City | Decca, reissued MCA |
| 1968 | Loretta Lynn's Greatest Hits | Decca, reissued MCA |
| 1969 | Your Squaw Is On the Warpath | Decca, reissued MCA |
| 1969 | If We Put Our Heads Together (with Ernest Tubb) | Decca |

| YEAR | ALBUM | LABEL |
|------|-------|-------|
| 1969 | Woman of the World (To Make a Man) | Decca, reissued MCA |
| 1970 | Here's Loretta Singing "Wings Upon Your Horns" | Decca |
| 1970 | Loretta Lynn Writes 'Em and Sings 'Em | Decca, reissued MCA |
| 1971 | Coal Miner's Daughter | Decca, reissued MCA |
| 1971 | We Only Make Believe (with Conway Twitty) | Decca, reissued MCA |
| 1971 | I Wanna Be Free | Decca, reissued MCA |
| 1971 | You're Looking at Country | Decca, reissued MCA |
| 1972 | Lead Me On (with Conway Twitty) | Decca, reissued MCA |
| 1972 | One's On the Way | Decca, reissued MCA |
| 1972 | God Bless America Again | Decca, reissued MCA |
| 1972 | Alone With You | Vocalion, reissued Coral |
| 1972 | Here I Am Again | Decca, reissued MCA |
| 1973 | Entertainer of the Year | Decca, reissued MCA |
| 1973 | The Ernest Tubb and Loretta Lynn Story | MCA |
| 1973 | Louisiana Woman/Mississippi Man (with Conway Twitty) | MCA |
| 1973 | Love Is the Foundation | MCA |
| 1974 | Greatest Hits Volume II | MCA |

| YEAR | ALBUM | LABEL |
| --- | --- | --- |
| 1974 | Country Partners (with Conway Twitty) | MCA |
| 1974 | They Don't Make 'Em Like My Daddy | MCA |
| 1975 | Back to Country | MCA |
| 1975 | Feelings (with Conway Twitty) | MCA |
| 1975 | Home | MCA |
| 1976 | When the Tingle Becomes a Chill | MCA |
| 1976 | United Talent (with Conway Twitty) | MCA |
| 1976 | Somebody Somewhere | MCA |
| 1977 | I Remember Patsy | MCA |
| 1977 | Dynamic Duo (with Conway Twitty) | MCA |
| 1978 | Out of My Head and Back in My Bed | MCA |
| 1978 | Honky-Tonk Heroes (with Conway Twitty) | MCA |
| 1979 | We've Come a Long Way Baby | MCA |
| 1979 | The Very Best of Conway Twitty and Loretta Lynn | MCA |
| 1979 | Diamond Duet (with Conway Twitty) | MCA |
| 1981 | Loretta | MCA |
| 1981 | Looking Good | MCA |
| 1981 | Two's a Party (with Conway Twitty) | MCA |
| 1982 | I Lie | MCA |
| 1983 | Lyin' Cheatin' Woman Chasin' Honky-Tonkin' Whiskey-Drinkin' You | MCA |

| YEAR | SINGLE | LABEL | C&W | POP |
|------|--------|-------|-----|-----|
| 1960 | I'm a Honky-Tonk Girl | Zero | | |
| 1961 | The Girl That I Am Now | Decca | * | |
| 1962 | Success | Decca | | |
| 1962 | A World of Forgotten People | Decca | | |
| 1963 | The Other Woman | Decca, reissued MCA | | |
| 1963 | Before I'm Over You | Decca | * | |
| 1964 | Wine, Women and Song | Decca | * | |
| 1964 | Mr. and Mrs. Used To Be (with Ernest Tubb) | Decca | | |
| 1964 | Happy Birthday | Decca | * | |
| 1965 | Blue Kentucky Girl | Decca | * | |
| 1965 | Our Hearts Are Holding Hands | Decca | | |
| 1965 | The Home You're Tearin' Down | Decca | * | |
| 1965 | When I Hear My Children Pray | Decca | | |
| 1965 | Dear Uncle Sam | Decca, reissued MCA | * | |
| 1966 | You Ain't Woman Enough | Decca, reissued MCA | * | |
| 1966 | Don't Come Home A Drinkin' (With Lovin' On Your Mind) | Decca, reissued MCA | * | |
| 1966 | To Heck With Santa Claus | Decca | | |
| 1967 | Sweet Thing (with Ernest Tubb) | Decca, reissued MCA | | |
| 1967 | If You're Not Gone Too Long | Decca | * | |
| 1967 | A Man I Hardly Know | Decca | | |
| 1967 | What Kind of Girl (Do You Think I Am) | Decca | * | |
| 1968 | Fist City | Decca | * | |
| 1968 | You've Just Stepped In (From Stepping Out On Me) | Decca | * | |
| 1968 | Your Squaw Is On the Warpath | Decca, reissued MCA | * | |

| YEAR | SINGLE | LABEL | C&W | POP |
|------|--------|-------|-----|-----|
| 1969 | Woman of the World (Leave My World Alone) | Decca | * | |
| 1969 | To Make a Man (Feel Like a Man) | Decca | * | |
| 1969 | Somewhere Between (with Ernest Tubb) | Decca | | |
| 1969 | If We Put Our Heads Together (with Ernest Tubb) | Decca | | |
| 1969 | Wings Upon Your Horns | Decca | | |
| 1970 | I Know How | Decca | * | |
| 1970 | You Wanna Give Me a Lift | Decca | * | |
| 1970 | Coal Miner's Daughter | Decca, reissued MCA | * | x |
| 1971 | After The Fire Is Gone (with Conway Twitty) | Decca, reissued MCA | | x |
| 1971 | I Wanna Be Free | Decca, reissued MCA | * | x |
| 1971 | You're Looking at Country | Decca, reissued MCA | * | |
| 1971 | Lead Me On (with Conway Twitty) | Decca, reissued MCA | | |
| 1971 | One's On the Way | Decca, reissued MCA | * | |
| 1972 | Here I Am Again | Decca | * | |
| 1972 | Rated X | Decca, reissued MCA | * | |
| 1973 | Love Is the Foundation | MCA | * | |
| 1973 | Living Together Alone (with Conway Twitty) | MCA | | |

* Smash Hit
X Crossover to Pop

| YEAR | SINGLE | LABEL | C&W | POP |
|------|--------|-------|-----|-----|
| 1973 | Hey Loretta | MCA | * | |
| 1974 | They Don't Make 'Em Like My Daddy | MCA | * | |
| 1974 | As Soon As I Hang Up the Phone (with Conway Twitty) | MCA | * | |
| 1974 | Trouble in Paradise | MCA | * | |
| 1974 | Shadrack the Black Reindeer | MCA | | |
| 1975 | The Pill | MCA | * | x |
| 1975 | Home | MCA | * | |
| 1975 | When the Tingle Becomes a Chill | MCA | | |
| 1976 | Red, White and Blue | MCA | | |
| 1976 | The Letter (with Conway Twitty) | MCA | * | |
| 1976 | Feelings (with Conway Twitty) | MCA | * | |
| 1976 | Somebody Somewhere (Don't Know What He's Missing Tonight) | MCA | * | |
| 1977 | She's Got You | MCA | * | |
| 1977 | I Can't Love You Enough (with Conway Twitty) | MCA | * | |
| 1977 | Why Can't He Be You | MCA | * | |
| 1977 | Out of My Head and Back in My Bed | MCA | * | |
| 1978 | Spring Fever | MCA | | |
| 1978 | From Seven Till Ten (with Conway Twitty) | MCA | * | |
| 1978 | We've Come a Long Way Baby | MCA | * | |
| 1979 | I Can't Feel You Anymore | MCA | * | |
| 1979 | I've Got a Picture of Us On My Mind | MCA | * | |
| 1979 | You Know Just What I'd Do/The Sadness of It All (with Conway Twitty) | MCA | * | |
| 1980 | Pregnant Again | MCA | | |
| 1980 | Cheatin' On a Cheater | MCA | | |

| YEAR | SINGLE | LABEL | C&W | POP |
|------|--------|-------|-----|-----|
| 1981 | Lovin' What Your Lovin' Does To Me (with Conway Twitty) | MCA | | |
| 1981 | Somebody Led Me Away | MCA | | |
| 1981 | I Still Believe in Waltzes (with Conway Twitty) | MCA | | |
| 1982 | I Lie | MCA | * | |
| 1982 | Makin' Love From Memory | MCA | | |
| 1983 | Breakin' It/There's All Kinds of Smoke (In the Barroom) | MCA | | |
| 1983 | Lyin' Cheatin' Woman Chasin' Honky-Tonkin' Whiskey-Drinkin' You | MCA | | |

* Smash Hit
X Crossover to Pop

Willie Nelson—a country music original.

*I still think me and everybody else feel the same way about practically everything.*

Willie Nelson, Esquire

The best performers in American popular music have always been identified by their own unique mix of styles rather than by any particular category. Although Willie Nelson is a bona fide country music superstar, he has broken just about every rule that an aspiring performer needs to heed to try to reach the top.

Nelson doesn't sound like any other country singer. For years, record companies thought of Willie as a great songwriter who couldn't sing. When they finally let him record, they tried to hide his voice behind overblown instrumental backgrounds. Actually, the lack of polish in Willie's voice is one of the things that makes it so special. When he sings, you feel like you are listening to a wise old friend who is telling you about his travels. No matter what kind of song he is singing—and he has recorded everything from gospel hymns to ballads from the forties to cowboy laments—he always maintains that same earthy, human feeling that gets right down to the heart of the matter. When you hear one of Willie's records, you know who the singer is and that every note and word come right from the heart.

Willie Nelson doesn't look like any other country star. With his long Indian braids, wrinkled, bearded face, and the diamond stud he wears in one ear, Willie doesn't look like a pop star at all. If you didn't know any better, you might just think he was an over-the-hill hippie or a hawker of American-Indian souvenirs on some hot and dusty highway in the Southwest. Who would ever guess that this gritty-looking, fifty-year-old man is one of America's most important stars. A singer whose records cross all boundaries of audience appeal; an actor with a natural presence who is as comfortable on a movie set as he is on the concert stage; a personality so magnetic that a clothes designer has even started marketing jeans with his name on them.

Yes, Willie Nelson is all these things and a whole lot more. In an era that favors glitter and glamour, Willie comes across as the kind of guy with whom you could sit down and swap stories rather than some distant pop star who lives in his own world. Although he has become a very rich man, Willie makes a point of staying close to his audience. During an interview with *Musician* magazine, he remarked:

> *I simply have the desire to be that way, (and) that's all it takes, which doesn't mean that I also don't travel by private lear [jet]. . . . But I do not want to be separated from the people I'm trying to communicate with. . . . Those people out there are all friends of mine at the moment, and if I stayed in Ames, Iowa, last night, that crowd and I could have gotten along famously for years and years. Same thing in Minneapolis tonight: there*

*will be thousands of people in the audience I could hang out with without feeling at all uncomfortable.*

Willie Nelson fits into no mold or established category. He is someone who lives his life and creates his music on nothing less than his own terms.

## The Early Years

Willie Nelson was born on April 30, 1933, in the tiny town of Abbott, Texas (population 300), just north of Waco. By the time he was two, Willie's parents separated. His mother, Myrtle, moved north to Oregon, while his father, Ira, relocated in nearby Fort Worth. This left Willie and his sister, Bobbie, to be brought up by their grandparents, Mamma and Daddy Nelson.

Mamma Nelson took mail-order music lessons and wrote quite a few gospel songs. Shortly before his death, Daddy Nelson bought the five-year-old Willie his first guitar and showed him some basic chords. Even at that very young age, Willie began to soak up all kinds of musical influences. From the old wooden Philco radio that was in his grandparents' den, Willie heard broadcasts of the Grand Ole Opry along with the pop standards of the day. He also heard a good deal of Mexican music and black blues during occasional stints picking cotton. Although Willie's music reflects all the influences of his early years, he remembers being most impressed by the songs of the black fieldworkers:

"I first heard the blues picking cotton in a field full of black people," he told *Esquire* magazine. "One would sing a line at this end of the field, another one at that end. I realized they knew more about music, soul, and feeling than I did. Plus they could pick more cotton."

Willie's professional debut as a musician was not playing country, pop, or blues. At age nine, Willie had his first paying job with John Ray's Polka Band. "There were a lot of (Polish) and Czechoslovakian people down there," he recalls. "Playing with no amplification, with all those tubas and trombones and drums, there was no way anyone could really hear me, so I could make my mistakes young without being noticed."

During Willie's freshman year in high school, he was recruited into a band that included his sister Bobbie on piano, his father on fiddle, and his football coach on trombone. The band was lead by Bobbie's husband, who played bass and booked the jobs.

"Bobbie was the only one who was any good," Willie told writer Lola Scobey. "We never played the same place twice. We used to play on percentage, and I remember one night we cleared eighty-one cents each."

In spite of their musical deficiencies, the band often

gave live performances on the radio, and before long, Willie and Bobbie became local celebrities. "When I found myself singing over the radio," Willie recalls, "I didn't think life got much better than that."

Mamma Nelson was not too happy about her grandchildren playing in honky-tonks and bars all over the area, but there was little the aging woman could do, especially with Willie's father and high-school coach being band members. Mama Nelson had tried to teach her grandchildren to be religious, God-fearing Christians, but she soon realized that as far as Willie was concerned, she was fighting an uphill battle.

"I was playing some nightclubs in a town six miles away on Saturday nights," Willie told *Musician* magazine. "(Then) I'd go to church in Abbott on Sunday morning and find myself playing to the same crowds. I didn't tell the priest where they were the night before, and they didn't tell him where I was."

In spite of Willie's early introduction to the bars and the honky-tonks, he still found time to be a star athlete in high school and managed to graduate with a B average. He was even encouraged to try out for an athletic scholarship at Fort Worth's Weatherford Junior College, but he was unwilling to give up the musical jobs that kept him out until the wee hours of the morning. Instead, Willie joined the Air Force. But Willie's timing was bad. The armed forces were gearing up for the Korean War, and the regimentation of the military life did not suit a young man accustomed to coming and going as he pleased. After a few months, Willie suddenly developed back problems and was soon discharged from military service.

Now eighteen and without any real career plans, Willie married a sixteen-year-old carhop named Martha. "She was a full-blooded Cherokee (Indian)," Willie told *People* magazine. "And every night with us was like Custer's last stand. We'd live in one place for a month, then pick up and move when the rent would come due."

Within a few short years, Willie had three children to support. He tried to make ends meet by selling encyclopedias and Bibles door to door. He also worked as a janitor, a plumber's helper, and a disc jockey. Willie picked up a few extra dollars playing the local bars. Some of the places he played were so rough that chicken-wire fences were put up to protect the band from bottles and chairs that were thrown around.

At this point, there was no reason for anyone to expect that Willie could ever make a decent living in the music business, much less achieve the kind of recognition that has come to him in the last few years. Still, he had received some encouragement about his songwriting and was led to believe that there might be a market for his songs in that hotbed of country music, Nashville.

## Writing Blues and Paying Dues

Willie had started writing poems when he was a youngster. With a few chords his grandfather showed him and the sounds coming over the radio, Willie began to develop melodies for his poems. During his early twenties, Willie felt that he was finally making progress as a songwriter. Some of his tunes were being requested at local clubs, and he had even received a few offers to sell some of his songs outright.

If there's one mistake in the music business akin to selling your birthright, it has to be selling your song outright. Normally, a songwriter gets a percentage every time a recording of a song he or she writes is played or sold. But when you sell the rights to your song, you never see another penny, no matter how much it sells. During the fifties and early sixties, it was common for young, naive, and hungry songwriters to sell their tunes for a little bit of cash. Desperate to put food in the mouths of his family, Willie sold one of his songs, "Family Bible," for $50. In order to finance his trip to Nashville, Willie sold his most famous song, "Night Life," for $150.

It had cost him more than he was able to grasp, but Willie Nelson had arrived in what seemed to be the perfect place for a man of his talents. The opportunities in Nashville were many for a songwriter with a suitcase full of country tunes. In 1960, Claude

Gray's version of "Family Bible" became a top-ten hit. Unfortunately, Willie's excitement was quickly dulled when he realized that he wasn't going to earn any money from the success of that tune. Still, he had a hit song to his credit, and people were beginning to take notice.

Although Willie was about to hit a low point in his personal life, his career finally started to take off. Only a few months after arriving in Nashville, Willie had penned three top-ten hits: "Crazy," sung by Patsy Cline; "Hello Walls," recorded by Faron Young; and "Funny How the Time Slips Away," sung by Billy Walker. Even though he was earning money from his songwriting, Willie just hung out in bars and drank up the profits. Meanwhile, his wife Martha was working full-time as a bartender. Their frequent fights were getting more violent. Shortly before she left him, Martha rescued Willie from committing suicide. She found him drunk, lying down in the middle of the street in front of Tootsie's bar, waiting for a car to run him over. After she pulled him out of the gutter, Martha left Willie in a highly dramatic fashion.

"I came home drunk," he recalls, "and while I was passed out, she sewed me up in a sheet. Then she got a broomstick and started beating . . . me. . . . By the time I got loose, she'd lit out in the car with the kids, her clothes and *my* clothes. There was no way I could follow her naked and that was kind of the end of it."

Willie doesn't like to talk about the forces that were driving him to such a terrible emotional state. But whatever they were, he was really going through a rough time in his life.

"I was having so much domestic trouble," Willie told *Musician* magazine, "I didn't have the time to care about my career. I was going through a divorce and that lasted and lasted . . . and cost and cost. . . . The money I was making off my songwriting either went for booze or lawyers. There was a several-year period that was just a blur."

Personal problems and financial woes aside, Willie was getting somewhere as a hit songwriter in Nashville. The only thing was, he didn't feel satisfied just writing songs for other people. Willie had his own ideas about what he wanted his music to sound like, and that meant not only singing the songs himself, but assuming creative control of his recordings. This didn't go over well with the record executives in Nashville. Although he did record one country hit, "Touch Me," in 1962, it would be another thirteen years until he reached the top ten again.

During those years, Willie recorded for several labels, but most of his releases were either poorly promoted or poorly produced. Most of the early producers thought Willie was a bad singer, and they tried to get around this by covering his voice up with slick country playing and overbearing string arrangements. Willie summed up the problem for *Time* magazine this way: "I was trying to sell a new style of singer and they didn't have a category to put me in."

During this period, Willie entered into his second marriage with country singer Shirley Collie. He performed and recorded several albums with her. At one point, Willie quit the road, and he and Shirley turned their attention to raising hogs on a sprawling farm outside of Nashville. But Willie quickly discovered that he wasn't cut out to be a farmer. "We were buying hogs for twenty-seven cents a pound and selling them for seventeen," he told *Newsweek.* "Songwriting was better than that."

As the sixties came to a close, Willie's personal problems were getting the best of him again. "In 1969, I had gone through a divorce and had wrecked four cars," he recalls. "Hank Cochran and I had been sitting in the basement writing songs. . . . We were kicking all this around and ended up writing 'What Can You Do To Me Now.' The next day my house burned down."

## The Outlaw and Progressive Country Music

Even as Willie Nelson salvaged his precious Martin acoustic guitar from the flames, he had a feeling that this was one of those tragedies that people sometimes need in order to get on with their lives. Willie had been on a treadmill in Nashville for a decade. It was clear that he did not fit in with the established image of a country performer. Although he recorded about twenty albums during those years, including a few great ones, they were all commercial flops. Willie knew that it was time to move on and, as they say in show biz, get his act together. He moved to Texas, determined to play and record his kind of country music.

"(I needed some time to) concentrate and get some plan together," he told writer Joe Nick Patoski. "I knew this was probably my last shot . . . as far as selling a lot of records. . . . When you hit forty, for a picker, it's gettin' pretty close."

Willie soon bought a used Greyhound bus and started working that same circuit of clubs and honky-tonks in the Southwest that he had come to know so well. Although he was frustrated at his inability to break through as a performer during his Nashville years, Willie believed that he had something valuable and unique to offer. He also sensed an expanding audience for his kind of music. "I found a lot of interest in country music among young people," he recalls. "Their hair was often too long to get them into some of those (country music) places without getting into trouble . . . but I knew there was an audience there."

For the first time in his career, Willie felt that there was an opportunity for him to create his own market.

It was during this period that Willie grew his beard and famous braids, a look that would have been taboo in Nashville, but one which he thought captured the spirit of his new, expanded audience—an audience that included traditional country fans, rock and rollers with long hair, and college kids.

By 1971, Willie had signed on with Atlantic records in New York and recorded *Shotgun Willie,* the first album to capture the true feeling of a live Willie Nelson performance. In Atlantic's Jerry Wexler, Willie had at last found a record executive who appreciated his vocal talents. Wexler has often compared Willie's

Waylon Jennings—another "country outlaw" and frequent Nelson collaborator.

singing to that of Ray Charles, Billie Holliday, and Frank Sinatra, acknowledged giants of vocal artistry.

Willie also developed close ties with Waylon Jennings, Kris Kristofferson, and other talented country artists who also didn't fit the Nashville mold. In time, these artists would be considered the founders of a new *progressive* country music. But in the early seventies, they were called outlaws.

"When I left Nashville . . . I became a rebel," Willie told *Musician* magazine. "But it was when I made that cut, that split from the establishment, that made me a big 'outlaw.' You just didn't do that; you just didn't leave the store."

Now that Willie had finally recorded a good album that also sold well—*Shotgun Willie* had racked up more sales than all of his Nashville albums combined—and greatly expanded the audience for country music, he decided to come up with a unique forum for his music. On July 4, 1972, Willie staged the first of his annual picnics in Dripping Springs, Texas. Over 50,000 people showed up to hear Willie, Leon Russell, Waylon Jennings, Tom T. Hall, and Kris Kristofferson, in what was to become country music's most highly publicized annual event. These Fourth of July picnics turned out to be very important to Willie's future success.

"We found each other, artist and audience, and started growing together," Willie told *Look* magazine.

As his career grew, Willie's picnics became important national news. In 1980, after organizing his eighth picnic on his own country club near Austin, Willie decided that he no longer had the time and energy to stage these annual events. "It takes about six months to put one together, and afterwards about another six months to get over it," he explained. "I'd like to rest a while, but after that—we'll see."

Willie admits that one of the main purposes for staging his annual picnics was to sell the public on his

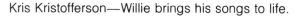

Kris Kristofferson—Willie brings his songs to life.

own music. In his years as a door-to-door salesman, Willie learned that "whatever you sell, you've got to sell yourself first." By 1976, Willie had not only sold himself, but many of his fellow Nashville "outlaws" as well.

An RCA album called *The Outlaws*, featuring Willie, Waylon Jennings, Tompall Glaser, and Jessi Colter, became the largest-selling country album up to that point. Willie and Waylon won three CMA awards in 1976: Best Vocal Duo, Best Single, and Best Album of the Year. In addition, five more of Willie's singles became top-ten country hits that year. The former country outlaw had become a primary reason why country music grew from a regional music form to one that now has devoted followers in all parts of America.

## A Man for All Music

Willie Nelson has often been called a "white Ray Charles." What a thrill it must be for a man whose voice record producers once considered unsuitable to be compared to one of the great vocal talents of our time. Like Ray Charles, Willie is a versatile singer, but his greatness lies not so much in vocal techniques as in his unique style and the human, down-to-earth quality he brings to whatever he sings. Unlike Ray Charles, Willie Nelson is not a singer whom a lot of people can imitate. If there is anything aspiring vocalists can learn from him, it would be to absorb as much music as possible and sing it as honestly as one can. In a way, Willie's voice is a rather modest instrument, yet the way he uses it to bring different kinds of music to life is ingenious. He can sing one of his own tunes, a pop standard like "Stardust," or a rock classic like Paul Simon's "Bridge Over Troubled Water" as if there were no differences at all in those songs. And to Willie, there really *are* no differences; it's all just music.

"When I started to work clubs around Texas," Willie told *High Fidelity* magazine, "songs (like) 'Stardust' were requested right along with (country standards like) 'San Antonio Rose,' and (polkas like) 'Fraulien.' The people I was singing to in the beer joints and clubs didn't know about labels like pop and country. All they liked were songs and music."

If you want to hear some good old American music, just pick up a Willie Nelson album. Try *Stardust* or *Somewhere Over The Rainbow* if you're in the mood for pop standards. If you're riding down a highway some night and you want to hear an album that combines country standards with some of Willie's best tunes, try listening to *Red-Headed Stranger,* a record which *Rolling Stone's* Chet Flippo called, "(a work) of such awesome depth and impact that I still find it hard to believe it's only a record." And if you think Kris Kristofferson is a good songwriter, you may not realize just how good he is until you've heard *Willie Nelson Sings Kristofferson*. If songs about love and marriage are what you're in the mood for, pick up a copy of the *Phases and Stages* album, in which Willie takes a look at that subject from both the man's and woman's point of view. And this is only the beginning. You wouldn't want to miss his great collaborations with Waylon Jennings, and Merle Haggard or the *Willie Nelson Live* album.

As you listen to Willie's music, you might not be aware of all the influences that shape it. But those notes and phrases that he plays on that beat-up old Martin acoustic guitar owe more to jazz greats like Les Paul and D'jango Reinhardt than to anyone from the country and western school of picking. The way Willie hesitates when he phrases a vocal line comes from the blues singers he heard as a boy. And the musical feel of his records can conjure up the mood of the haunted cowboy that lives somewhere in his soul or the Mexican neighbors who lived down the street when he was growing up in Abbott, Texas.

When Willie talks about his own musical tastes, he mentions jazz, country, blues, and polkas almost in the same breath. To Willie, his mixing of various influences is a unique and positive aspect of his music. He refutes the notion of some critics that if music draws from a wide range of influences and reaches a wide number of people, then it must somehow be compromised or watered down.

"I don't think I'm watered down," he told *Musician* magazine. "I'm very sincere. I may not play as good jazz as Miles Davis, or as good blues as B.B. King, or as good country as (some singers) . . . but I enjoy what I do. . . . (My music) is a mixture. Any listeners completely under the sway of one type of music are going to be disappointed in what they hear from me, 'cause I come from a lot of different places."

## On the Road with Willie Nelson

In ten short years, Willie Nelson has gone from country outlaw to national superstar. Aside from his music career, which has evolved to the point of playing mostly large indoor stadiums, Willie is also a highly acclaimed film star with movies like *Barbarosa, Honeysuckle Rose,* and *The Electric Horseman* under his belt and several more in the works. He has sung at the White House and jogged with former President Jimmy Carter. He has already recorded duet albums with Roger Miller and Webb Pierce, Merle Haggard and Waylon Jennings, and is discussing future projects with Bob Dylan and Ray Charles.

Despite all of his recording and film projects, Willie still sees his main calling as a live performer. "I enjoy (acting) very much," Willie told the *Journal of Country Music*. "But I think I'd get restless if I had to do it forever. Movies are fun, but they are also a little confining. You can't get up and go somewhere every day . . . and that goes against my grain a little bit. Mainly, I'm going to continue playing music because that's what I really know how to do, and what I enjoy more than anything else in the world."

These days, Willie and his "family" of twenty-five musicians and roadies travel and perform about 250 days a year. Although he makes more than enough money to take planes, Willie insists on traveling by bus. "I rest better because there's no phone," he told *People* magazine. "And traveling is a big part of my life. I haven't seen much of the country, but I've been all over it a thousand times, just lying in the back with the blinds drawn. I guess it's the perpetual motion I like."

Willie's band, which includes sister Bobbie on piano, is an important part of his sound. They follow him through endless turns of melody and rhythm just as they follow him to the small towns and big cities where he performs. The atmosphere between Willie and his extended family is quite loose. Yet they are total professionals when they hit the stage. Willie and his band have a reputation for starting on time and delivering much more than is expected of them.

It is this combination of professional and personal contact that makes Willie Nelson such a charismatic live performer. The highlight of his set—which often runs to between fifty and sixty songs—is the traditional hymn, "Amazing Grace":

*Amazing grace, how sweet the sound,*
*    To save a wretch like me.*
*I once was lost, but now I'm found,*
*    Was blind, but now I see.*

During this song, Willie's devoted fans light candles and shower him with flowers. Willie responds by throwing his bandana into the crowd. No wonder Willie Nelson concerts are often referred to as "spiritual experiences."

After the show ends, Willie might spend another two hours signing autographs. Unlike some stars, Willie's trademark is that he is always accessible to his fans. "He just can't say no to anybody," his third wife Connie told *People* magazine. "I've seen Willie get so tired he can't go any further. Then someone will ask one more thing from him and he'll do it. He doesn't ever want anybody to think that success has changed him."

# Willie Nelson Collector's Guide

| YEAR | ALBUM | LABEL |
|------|-------|-------|
| 1962 | And Then I Wrote | Liberty |
| 1963 | Here's Willie Nelson | Liberty |
| 1965 | Country Willie—His Own Songs | RCA |
| 1966 | Country Favorites—Willie Nelson Style | RCA |
| 1966 | Country Music Concert—Willie Nelson | RCA |
| 1966 | Hello Walls | Sunset |
| 1967 | Make Way for Willie Nelson | RCA |
| 1967 | The Party's Over | RCA |
| 1968 | Texas in My Soul | RCA |
| 1968 | Good Ol' Country Singin' | CAL |
| 1968 | Good Times | RCA |
| 1969 | My Own Peculiar Way | RCA |
| 1970 | Both Sides Now (Sweet Memories) | RCA |
| 1970 | Laying My Burdens Down | RCA |
| 1970 | Columbus Stockade Blues | CAF |
| 1971 | Willie Nelson and Family | RCA |
| 1971 | Yesterday's Wine | RCA |
| 1972 | The Words Don't Fit the Pictures | RCA |
| 1972 | The Willie Way | RCA |
| 1973 | The Best of Willie Nelson | U.A. |
| 1973 | Country Winners by Willie | Camden |
| 1973 | Shotgun Willie | Atlantic |
| 1974 | Spotlight on Willie Nelson | Camden |
| 1974 | Phases and Stages | Atlantic |
| 1975 | Red-Headed Stranger | Columbia |
| 1975 | Willie Nelson and His Friends | Plantation |
| 1975 | What Can You Do To Me | RCA |
| 1975 | Country Willie | U.A. |

| YEAR | ALBUM | LABEL |
| --- | --- | --- |
| 1976 | The Outlaws (with Waylon Jennings) | RCA |
| 1976 | The Sound in Your Mind | Columbia |
| 1976 | Columbus Stockade Blues and Other Country Favorites | Camden |
| 1976 | Willie Nelson Live | RCA |
| 1976 | The Troublemaker | Columbia |
| 1977 | Willie Before His Time | RCA |
| 1977 | To Lefty from Willie | Columbia |
| 1977 | Willie Nelson—1961 | Shotgun |
| 1978 | Hello Walls | Pickwick |
| 1978 | Waylon And Willie (with Waylon Jennings) | RCA |
| 1978 | Stardust | Columbia |
| 1978 | Face of a Fighter | Lonestar |
| 1978 | There'll Be No Teardrops Tonight | U.A. |
| 1978 | Willie and Family Live | Columbia |
| 1979 | Help Me Make It Through the Night | Columbia |
| 1979 | Sweet Memories | RCA |
| 1979 | One For the Road (with Leon Russel) | Columbia |
| 1979 | Willie Nelson Sings Kristofferson | Columbia |
| 1979 | Pretty Paper (with Leon Russel) | Columbia |
| 1980 | Danny Davis and Willie Nelson (with the Nashville Brass) | RCA |
| 1980 | San Antonio Rose (with Ray Price) | Columbia |
| 1980 | Honeysuckle Rose (Soundtrack) | Columbia |
| 1980 | Family Bible (with Danny Davis and the Nashville Brass and Ray Price) | Songbird |
| 1980 | Electric Horseman (soundtrack) | Columbia |

| YEAR | ALBUM | LABEL |
|---|---|---|
| 1981 | Minstrel Man | RCA |
| 1981 | Somewhere Over the Rainbow | Columbia |
| 1981 | Greatest Hits and Some That Be | Columbia |
| 1982 | Always On My Mind | Columbia |
| 1982 | The Best of Willie | RCA |
| 1982 | W.W.II (with Waylon Jennings) | RCA |
| 1982 | Kris, Willie, Dolly and Brenda . . . The Winning Hand (with Kris Kristofferson, Dolly Parton and Brenda Lee) | Monument |
| 1983 | Poncho and Lefty (with Merle Haggard) | Columbia |
| 1983 | Tougher Than Leather | Columbia |
| 1983 | Take It To the Limit (with Waylon Jennings) | Columbia |

| YEAR | SINGLE | LABEL | C&W | POP |
|---|---|---|---|---|
| 1962 | Willingly (with Shirley Collie) | Liberty | * | |
| 1962 | Touch Me | Liberty | * | |
| 1963 | Half a Man | Liberty | | |
| 1964 | You Took My Happy Away | Liberty | | |
| 1965 | She's Not For You | RCA | | |
| 1965 | I Just Can't Let You Say Goodbye | RCA | | |
| 1966 | One In a Row | RCA | | |
| 1967 | The Party's Over | RCA | | |
| 1967 | Blackjack Country Chain | RCA | | |
| 1967 | San Antonio | RCA | | |
| 1968 | Little Things | RCA | | |
| 1968 | Good Times | RCA | | |

| YEAR | SINGLE | LABEL | C&W | POP |
|------|--------|-------|-----|-----|
| 1968 | Johnny One Time | RCA | | |
| 1968 | Bring Me Sunshine | RCA | | |
| 1969 | I Hope So | Liberty | | |
| 1970 | Once More with Feeling | RCA | | |
| 1970 | Laying My Burdens Down | RCA | | |
| 1971 | I'm a Memory | RCA | | |
| 1971 | Yesterday's Wine/Me and Paul | RCA | | |
| 1972 | The Words Don't Fit the Picture | RCA | | |
| 1973 | Shotgun Willie | Atlantic | | |
| 1973 | Stay All Night | Atlantic | | |
| 1974 | I Still Can't Believe You're Gone | Atlantic | | |
| 1974 | Bloody Mary Morning | Atlantic | | |
| 1974 | Sister's Coming Home | Atlantic | | |
| 1974 | After the Fire Is Gone (with Tracy Nelson) | Atlantic | | |
| 1975 | Blue Eyes Crying in the Rain | Columbia | * | X |
| 1975 | Fire and Rain | RCA | | |
| 1976 | Remember Me | Columbia | * | X |
| 1976 | Good-Hearted Woman | Columbia | | X |
| 1976 | The Last Letter | U.A. | | |
| 1976 | I Gotta Get Drunk | RCA | | |
| 1976 | I'd Have To Be Crazy | Columbia | | |
| 1976 | If You've Got the Money I've Got the Time | Columbia | * | |
| 1976 | Uncloudy Day | Columbia | * | |
| 1977 | I'm a Memory | RCA | | |
| 1977 | I Love You a Thousand Ways | Lonestar | * | |
| 1977 | You Ought To Hear Me Cry | RCA | | |
| 1978 | Mammas Don't Let Your Babies Grow Up To Be Cowboys (with Waylon Jennings) | RCA | * | X |

* Smash Hit
X Crossover to Pop

**117**

| YEAR | SINGLE | LABEL | C&W | POP |
|------|--------|-------|-----|-----|
| 1978 | If You Can Touch Her at All | RCA | * | |
| 1978 | Georgia On My Mind | Columbia | * | x |
| 1978 | Blue Skies | Columbia | * | |
| 1978 | Ain't Life Hell (with Hank Cochran) | Capital | | |
| 1978 | All of Me | Columbia | * | |
| 1978 | Will You Remember Me | Lonestar | | |
| 1978 | There'll Be No Teardrops Tonight | U.A. | | |
| 1978 | Whiskey River | Columbia | | |
| 1979 | Sweet Memories | RCA | * | |
| 1979 | September Song | Columbia | | |
| 1979 | Heartbreak Hotel | Columbia | * | |
| 1979 | Crazy Arms | Columbia | | |
| 1979 | Help Me Make It Through the Night | Columbia | * | |
| 1980 | My Heroes Have Always Been Cowboys | Columbia | * | |
| 1980 | Night Life | RCA | | |
| 1980 | Midnight Rider | Columbia | * | |
| 1980 | Funny How Time Slips Away | RCA | | |
| 1980 | Faded Love | Columbia | * | |
| 1980 | On the Road Again | Columbia | * | |
| 1980 | Family Bible | Songbird | | |
| 1980 | Don't You Ever Get Tired of Hurting Me | Columbia | | |
| 1980 | Angel Flying Too Close To the Ground (with Ray Price) | Columbia | * | |
| 1980 | Heartaches of a Fool | Columbia | | |
| 1981 | Good Times | RCA | | |
| 1981 | My Heroes Have Always Been Cowboys | Columbia | | |
| 1981 | I'm Going To Sit Right Down and Write Myself a Letter | Columbia | | |

| YEAR | SINGLE | LABEL | C&W | POP |
|------|--------|-------|-----|-----|
| 1981 | Mountain Dew | Columbia | | |
| 1982 | (Sittin 'On) The Dock of the Bay (with Waylon Jennings) | RCA | | |
| 1982 | Just To Satisfy You (with Waylon Jennings) | RCA | * | |
| 1982 | Always On My Mind | Columbia | * | x* |
| 1982 | Old Friends (with Roger Miller and Ray Price) | Columbia | | |
| 1982 | Let It Be Me | Columbia | * | x |
| 1982 | In the Jailhouse Now (with Webb Pierce) | Columbia | | |
| 1982 | Last Thing I Needed First Thing this Morning | Columbia | * | |
| 1982 | Everything's Beautiful In Its Own Way (with Dolly Parton) | Monument | * | |
| 1983 | Reasons To Quit (with Merle Haggard) | Epic | * | |
| 1983 | A Little Old-Fashioned Karma | Columbia | | |
| 1983 | You're Gonna Love Yourself (In the Morning) (with Brenda Lee) | Monument | | |
| 1983 | Poncho and Lefty (with Merle Haggard) | Epic | * | |
| 1983 | Why Do I Have To Choose | Columbia | | |

* Smash Hit
X Crossover to Pop

Charley Pride—"pride of the South."

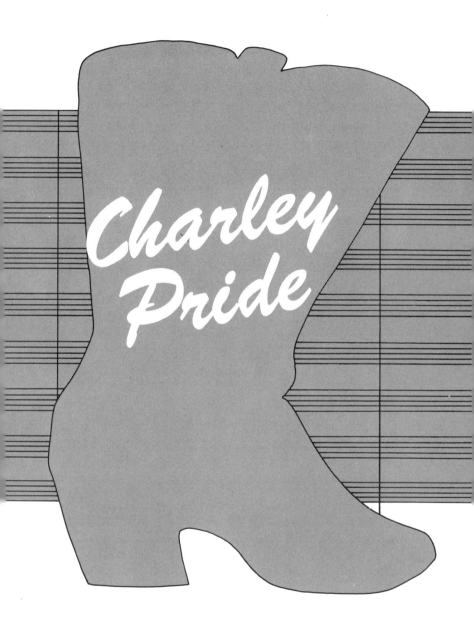

*My color says I'm supposed to shine shoes and sing the blues, but I don't fit that image, you see, because I'm Charley Pride, the man. I'm not a black man singing white man's music. I'm an American singing American music. I worked out those problems years ago—and everybody else will have to work their way out of it, too.*

Charley Pride, People

There are two great American musical traditions from which most of our popular styles are derived. One comes from the English-speaking settlers who immigrated from England, Scotland, and Ireland. The second great tradition has its origins in Africa and the black slaves who were shipped to these shores in chains. Although these slaves were forced to abandon their native languages and religions for those of their masters, the old African sounds and rhythms were never completely stamped out.

By the time the slaves were freed in 1865, there was all kinds of evidence that the once separate musical traditions were now permanently linked. The banjo —with origins in Africa—became one of the most popular instruments among white musicians in the South. Meanwhile, drifting black singers evolved a style called the blues. This uniquely American music drew its strength from both African and Anglican origins. From this single musical seed came jazz, rock and roll, rhythm and blues, and a number of country music styles as well.

Through the years, many country music stars have acknowledged their debt to black musicians. In some cases, these future stars were the children of poor sharecroppers who worked with blacks in the fields and picked up their music. In other instances, a young white musician would follow his black hero around in order to learn his tricks. Hank Williams, for example, always credited a black street singer named Tee-Tot for teaching him everything he knew. Young Jerry Lee Lewis and his cousin Mickey Gilley would sneak into black nightclubs to hear the great blues singers of the late forties and early fifties. When Elvis Presley started singing, he copied blues musicians like Big Boy Crudup and Big Bill Broonzy as well as country singers like Jimmy Rodgers and Ernest Tubb. To these youngsters growing up in the rural South, it was all just great music. There was no color line.

Although they may not have intended it, the young white musicians who allowed themselves to be strongly influenced by black styles were at the cutting edge of some important changes that began to take place in the South in the fifties. For years, country music was the expression of the southern white community, while the blues was called "race music," meaning music by and for blacks. But a new generation of musicians and listeners was demanding integration in their music. To some extent, this trend mirrored the civil rights movement, which was picking up steam at exactly the same time.

When rock and roll exploded in the mid-fifties, it was, in many ways, the full integration of the two great American musical traditions. Elvis Presley—who became the hottest entertainer America had ever seen—was known, among other things, as the "boy who stole the blues" and the first "white boy with a black sound" to make it big. It was clear that many teenagers of all races felt a greater bond among themselves than to the particular cultural group from which they came. Rock and roll cut across all barriers of culture and race. If you were young and could "dig" the feeling, the music belonged to you.

Some country music traditionalists did not appreciate this turn of events. Actually, it was another sign of the times in the fast-changing South. While the average southerner was relatively powerless in stemming the tide of integration, he or she did have a good deal of control over which records were bought. To many people, country music represented the values of the old South. A performer could lose a good part of the audience by taking the wrong political stance or even recording a song that moved too far away from established country music traditions. It was, however, too late to completely stem the tide. Musical integration was becoming a fact of life.

We have grown accustomed to hearing about white singers being influenced by black musical styles, although we rarely hear black singers paying the same kind of tribute to white traditions. This is particularly true in country music where until very recently, black performers were almost nonexistent. This despite the fact that Ray Charles—widely acknowledged as a giant of rhythm and blues and jazz—recorded one of the most important country albums of the sixties—*Modern Sounds In Country and Western Music.*

Ray Charles is perhaps the only performer in history who has made such a tremendous impact on so many musical styles. Yet many ardent country fans don't know that in 1946, he wore a white western suit and billed himself as the "only colored, singing cowboy." He moved away from country music until the *Modern Sounds . . .* album. Here again, because he was black, the tremendous importance of this groundbreaking album has been overlooked. This lack of recognition was cited by Loretta Lynn in her autobiography, *Coal Miner's Daughter*:

> *In my opinion, Ray Charles helped make country music more popular with more fans. . . . Ray Charles is black, and he's a soul singer. . . . And country music used to mean all white. But you think about it. How much difference is there between soul music and blues and some of our old-fashioned country songs? All of it is people letting their feelings out. . . . Ray Charles took*

*"our" songs and he gave a soul feeling to 'em. After hearing him, people were more prepared for Johnny Cash and Merle Haggard—and Loretta Lynn. Ray Charles made it easier for all of us to reach a bigger audience, and I don't feel he's ever gotten the credit he deserves from Nashville.*

We have taken the long way around in our look at Charley Pride because it is important to understand how difficult and unusual it is for a black man to

Ray Charles—one of country music's unsung heroes.

become a superstar of country music. As great a country singer as Ray Charles is, he did not attempt to record a country album until he was well established in other musical areas. For Charley Pride, however, country music was not one of several styles from which he could choose. If he was going to have a career in show business, it was going to be as a country singer and nothing else. People often talk about how much courage it took for Elvis to sing like a black blues singer. How much courage did it take for Charley Pride to attempt to make his mark by singing what most people regarded as music strictly by and for white people?

In many respects, Charley Pride grew up in circumstances that were identical to those of other country singers. Born in 1938 on the forty-acre Mississippi cotton farm his father sharecropped, Charley was one of eleven children. Although the Great Depression was over, there were many mouths to feed. Charley and his brothers and sisters started picking cotton at an early age. Like other families in that time and place, Charley's folks liked to gather round and listen to the radio after the long working day was over. Sometimes the Prides listened to broadcasts of the Grand Ole Opry. This in itself was not very unusual. But when young Charley began to show a genuine fascination with country music, his family became somewhat concerned. After all, they were living in

Sledge, Mississippi, right in the heart of the Mississippi Delta. This was an area that had nurtured many of the great rural blues singers. Not only did most southern blacks prefer the blues as music, they also took pride in the fact that it was an art form that belonged to them. It is not surprising, then, that Charley's love for country music did not sit well with many of his friends and relatives.

None of this really bothered Charley very much. When, at age fourteen, he saved enough money to buy a ten-dollar guitar, he fulfilled a long-standing dream. As he told an interviewer from *Sepia* magazine: "I opened it up, lifted it in my hands, and strummed my first chords. That minute I was the happiest kid in Mississippi." Like other future country music superstars, Charley dreamed that his guitar might be the ticket out of a life of picking cotton twelve hours a day. The fact that such dreams rarely amount to much, particularly when they belong to a black teenager in love with country music, apparently had little effect on him.

Charley had an even stronger dream floating around in his head. He was an outstanding baseball player who believed he could turn that skill into a profession. As Ann Malone points out in *The Stars of Country Music*, baseball and country music were dual interests Charley had in common with many white country boys. There were lots of good fields around for games, and the equipment required wasn't very expensive. Charley idolized the black baseball players like Jackie Robinson, Roy Campanella, and Satchel Paige. Baseball had become integrated in 1947, and Charley felt there was a real chance for him to break in. His family and friends tried to discourage him from pursuing his dream. In a sense, they were probably trying to protect him from being hurt and disappointed. But their negative words still must have been disheartening.

"When you are growing up and people keep telling you these (negative) things, you start believing them," Charley once told an interviewer. But ultimately he had the determination to try his luck. For ten years, beginning in 1954, Charley put everything he had into making it as a major-league baseball player.

Even today, after twenty years as an important country artist, Charley has not totally accepted the fact that he never made it as a big-league baseball player. He once made the following statement in the *New York Sunday News:*

*I love singing. Don't get me wrong, but I haven't got the slightest ambition to become the greatest singer in the world. I want to do well, but I don't want to try to outsing anyone or try to win every award.*

*Playing baseball is another matter. I wanted to be the greatest ballplayer that ever put on a uniform. I wanted people to know that Charley Pride hit more home runs than Babe Ruth and stole more bases than anyone. I wanted every record imaginable in the game.*

Although he was an outstanding hitter and pitcher in the Negro Leagues, he suffered an injury when he was twenty that prevented him from making it to the majors. Still, he kept pursuing his dream. He came closest in 1961 when the California Angels gave him a brief but unsuccessful tryout. Charley then spent some time working as a zinc smelter in Helena, Montana, while playing semi-professional ball. "Every once in a while I'd sing between innings and the crowd seemed to like it," Charley told Melvin Shestack, author of *The Country Music Encyclopedia:*

> *Some folks who had a nightclub heard me and soon I was playing baseball, smelting, and singing at nights. I thought it was a pretty good life. Then one night (country singer) Red Sovine came into the club, told me I should look him up in Nashville, but I wasn't ready. I (still) wanted to play for the majors . . . and decided to try out for the (New York) Mets. . . . (Mets manager Casey) Stengel didn't seem to know I was coming and I overheard him saying that he wasn't running a . . . tryout camp. They let me try out anyway, but I wasn't good enough.*

Thinking that perhaps this time his baseball career really was at an end, Charley decided to stop at Nashville on his way back to Montana and see what Red Sovine could line up for him. Sovine helped him make a tape and get it to record producer Jack Clement. "They liked the tape," Charley recalls in *The Country Music Encyclopedia,* "but they wanted me to dress up funny and bill me as George Washington III.... I told them that I wouldn't be no clown for nobody, that I was going to sing under my own name...."

Eventually, Charley's tape got to Chet Atkins, a top guitarist who had also produced some of Elvis Presley's early hits for RCA records. Atkins felt that Charley was good enough for RCA to sign to a recording contract. Now he had to convince the record company executives to take a chance with a black country singer. He described that meeting in *Esquire* magazine:

> *(I) brought the tape to a meeting of . . . all the top creative brass at RCA. I played (it) and everybody agreed he was worth signing up. Then I told them he was black. Pure silence. Finally, someone broke in, "He's great, though. Let's take a chance." And the rest is history. A lot of people believed that we were making a mistake, that disc jockeys in the deep South wouldn't play him. That he wouldn't get any promotion. They were wrong.*

Charley's first single on RCA—"Snakes Crawl at Night" and "Atlantic Coastal Line"—was released in December 1965. Although the record company had confidence in his talent, they were uncertain how country listeners would respond to a black performer. They decided to hedge their bets by not releasing the customary publicity photograph with the record. For months, radio stations played it and fans listened to Charley without knowing he was a black man. By the time they found out, they were hooked on his voice. Charley himself agreed with RCA's strategy.

"I knew that a lot of people were hung up on color in this country," he told the *New York Sunday News.* "And I realized that many of them wouldn't accept me if they realized I was black. When the record company decided to hide my color, I thought it was a good idea."

Charley's sound was so appealing that country fans quickly overcame any negative racial considerations. Because he understood the delicate situation he was in, Charley was careful not to do or say anything that would provoke any negative feelings. Charley is friendly and easygoing both on and off stage, and able to put white audiences at ease by making jokes about his "permanent tan." At over six feet, 190 pounds, Charley cuts an imposing figure in his immaculately tailored western suits. Although women find him very attractive, Charley makes it a point to stay away from hip-shaking gyrations and sexual overtones in his performances. As writer Ann Malone observes: "(Charley Pride) is about as clean-cut, affable, and inoffensive personally as any star in country music, and these characteristics were a great boon to his acceptance by white audiences."

In spite of his easygoing ways, however, Charley is sensitive about his unique racial situation. He doesn't especially like making jokes about his color any longer. After he firmly established himself as an important star of country music, he began eliminating these remarks from his performance.

"I kept saying that kind of thing for quite awhile until it wasn't necessary," he told *Newsweek* in 1973. "I mean now after nineteen albums, I don't have to say anything."

Although he is certainly sincere in his feelings, Charley is not about to start alienating the very people to whom he owes his popularity. For example, part of his stage act throughout the seventies included a version of the song, "Them Old Cotton Fields Back Home:"

*When I was a little bitty baby,*
*My Mama would rock me in the cradle,*
*In them old cotton fields back home*
*It was down in Louisiana*
*Just about a mile from Texarkana*
*In them old cotton fields back home*
*(chorus)*
*Now when them cotton balls get rotten*
*You can't pick very much cotton,*
*In them old cotton fields back home*

*It was down in Louisiana*
*Just about a mile from Texarkana*
*In them old cotton fields back home*

Charley always introduces the above song by telling the audience that working in the cotton fields is the kind of life from which he came, and he hopes never to go back to it. Ann Malone feels that Charley includes this routine for the purpose of "assuring racially conservative audiences that he is a Negro who knows who he is and where he comes from." Perhaps this kind of thinking does enter into the picture. But in all fairness, we cannot conclude that Charley Pride takes any greater care in fostering a particular image than many other country performers. It is well known that country music audiences are more sensitive to the personalities and views of their musical idols than any other fans. Why should Charley be expected to take any less care in molding his image than, for instance, Johnny Cash or Dolly Parton? The most important point is that he is a truly great country singer with a sincere love for the music he sings.

"I'm an individual who just happened to like the sound of this music," Charley told the *New York Sunday News*. "Ever since I was a kid, I've been listening to it and singing it. I just can't explain why I'm the first black to make it in this field."

Whatever the exact combination of reasons might be, Charley Pride certainly has made it big as a country singer. He has recorded over thirty albums for RCA. His awards—too numerous to list here—include: Best Male Country Vocalist and Artist of the Year (Country Music Association); Entertainer of the Year (Music Operators of America); Top Male Vocalist on Singles, and Top Male Vocalist on Albums (*Billboard* magazine); and Top Male Country Vocalist (*Cashbox* magazine). He has won all this in addition to several Grammy Awards, including Best Gospel Performance and Best Country Performance.

Unlike many other country music superstars, Charley does not write his own material. His strength lies in being an interperter of songs. Producer Chet Atkins has worked with many great singers and rates Charley as one of the very best. "Put Charley Pride on the worst PA (public address) system in the country and it doesn't matter," he told *Esquire*. "He'll penetrate. That's greatness. Few have it. Charley does."

Atkins likens Charley to Frank Sinatra in terms of being a great popular singer with that "certain intangible edge." However, Charley is most often compared to Hank Williams. Charley admits that Hank was one of his strongest influences. It is sometimes said that all singers learn their craft by imitating an older singer whom they idolize. If such is the case,

Hank was probably Charley's single greatest model. During the early stages of his career, Charley sang Williams's hits like "Lovesick Blues" and "Kaw-linga" well enough to move some observers to say that he eclipsed the original versions. More recently, he has moved away from songs that are identified with other singers to those that help forge his own strong identity.

Although Charley can yodel like Hank Williams, he usually sings in a smooth, rich baritone. His sound is so easy and effortless that people often overlook his amazing vocal range. He has long preferred songs about the South, and love songs like "Does My Ring Hurt Your Finger" and "Kiss an Angel Good Morning." In *The Country Music Encyclopedia*, Charley explained why he chooses to sing about these subjects:

*I feel music is just like buying or selling groceries, or insurance, or anything else. . . . The better the product you've got . . . the better you can sell it. . . . I have to really like a song. I have to feel that I can put my heart into it because I sing . . . from the heart.*

*Why do I (sing) mostly love songs? Well, I believe in love for one thing. And some of the songs I've recorded remind me not only of situations that other people have been in, but of situations that I've been in. And I just love ballads. I don't believe music should be used to promote politics, or religion, or whatever.*

Many of Charley's songs are upbeat and optimistic, and for good reason. He has made a great deal of money during the last twenty years and is financially secure. He also has a rich family life with his wife Rozene and their three children. Between recording sessions, concerts, and looking after his extensive real estate, song publishing, and radio interests, Charley doesn't get to spend as much time as he would like at his home in Dallas. Unlike some of his contemporaries, there have been no scandals and no headlines in gossip magazines.

Now that he is an established star, Charley is a familiar and welcome sight at practices of the Texas Rangers baseball team, with whom he works out when time permits. This country music superstar who started out as a baseball player has done extraordinarily well by any standards, although he may still feel that he missed his true calling as an athlete.

There is also the burden he must bear by forever being identified as the first important black man to make it in a "white man's music." Perhaps in some ways it is an honor to be called the "Jackie Robinson of country music." But one gets the impression that Charley Pride would much rather be thought of as a great country singer who just happens to be black. In recent years, other black country performers have surfaced, and they often credit Charley with helping make their success possible. Yet when black country singer Tony Edwards made an album in the early seventies and wrote in the liner notes: "I want to thank God and Charley Pride for making this possible," Charley was not moved.

"I didn't go into country music to break barriers for someone else," he told the *New York Sunday News.* "But if it happened, that's fine."

Charley doesn't like to talk about race issues much, just as he doesn't like to get involved in politics. He certainly realizes his unique position in the field of country music, but he doesn't want to focus on that part of his life. He would probably rather have people think of him as a country boy with ambition and talent who wanted to be a baseball player but wound up a country singer. If this is a profile that fits only him and no one else, that would probably also be okay with Charley Pride. "I was always sort of odd . . ." he told *Country Music* magazine, "because what I was doing . . . was trying to be an individual."

However Charley Pride chooses to think of himself, and no matter what he accomplishes in the years to come, he cannot escape the position he has forged for himself in the ongoing relationship between America's two great musical traditions. If Elvis Presley is remembered as the man who absorbed black musical styles and made them understandable to people around the world, how will history record the significance of Charley Pride? Musicologist Jules Siegel addressed this question in a letter to Melvin Shestack, which was printed in *Esquire* magazine. It said, in part:

> *Elvis Presley was a white country boy who sang with a black accent. The Beatles were white English boys who sang in the idiom of Presley and other white performers. Bob Dylan was a white poet who chose to combine the country voice with the black style. These performers have been translators standing between black and white; and explaining one side to the other. Until now, the black message has mainly flowed through white translators to the white audiences. Its effect has been overpoweringly great. . . .*
>
> *Charley Pride may not yet have chosen to deliver any special message, but he has proven that it is possible for a black man to sing in a white voice. When he or those who come after him begin to instruct as well as entertain . . . America will be changed forever.*

# Charley Pride Collector's Guide

| YEAR | ALBUM | LABEL |
|------|-------|-------|
| 1967 | Pride of Country Music | RCA Victor |
| 1968 | The Country Way | RCA Victor |
| 1968 | Make Mine Country | RCA Victor |
| 1968 | Songs of Pride | RCA Victor |
| 1969 | Charley Pride | RCA Victor |
| 1969 | Sensational | RCA Victor |
| 1969 | The Best of Charley Pride | RCA Victor |
| 1970 | Just Plain Charley | RCA Victor |
| 1970 | Charley Pride's 10th Album | RCA Victor |
| 1971 | From Me to You | RCA Victor |
| 1971 | Did You Think to Pray | RCA Victor |
| 1971 | I'm Just Me | RCA Victor |
| 1971 | Charley Pride Sings Heart Songs | RCA Victor |
| 1972 | The Best of Charley Pride Volume II | RCA Victor |
| 1972 | The Incomparable | RCA-Camden |
| 1972 | A Sunshiny Day | RCA |
| 1973 | Songs of Love | RCA |
| 1973 | Sweet Country | RCA |
| 1973 | Presents the Pridesman | RCA |
| 1973 | Amazing Love | RCA |
| 1974 | The Best of Charley Pride | RCA |
| 1975 | In Person (Panther Hall) | RCA |
| 1975 | Charley | RCA |
| 1976 | The Happiness of Having You | RCA |
| 1976 | Sunday Morning | RCA |
| 1976 | The Best of Charley Pride Volume III | RCA |
| 1977 | She's Just an Old Love Turned Memory | RCA |
| 1978 | Somebody Loves You Honey | RCA |

| YEAR | ALBUM | LABEL |
|------|-------|-------|
| 1978 | Burgers and Fries/When I Stop Leaving (I'll Be Gone) | RCA |
| 1979 | You're My Jamaica | RCA |
| 1980 | There's a Little Bit of Hank in Me | RCA |
| 1981 | Roll On Mississippi | RCA |
| 1981 | Greatest Hits | RCA |
| 1982 | Charley Sings Everybody's Choice | RCA |
| 1982 | Charley Pride Live | RCA |
| 1983 | Country Classics | RCA |
| 1983 | Night Games | RCA |

| YEAR | SINGLE | LABEL | C&W | POP |
|------|--------|-------|-----|-----|
| 1966 | Just Between You and Me | RCA | * | |
| 1967 | I Know One | RCA | * | |
| 1967 | Does My Ring Hurt Your Finger | RCA | * | |
| 1968 | The Day the Earth Stood Still | RCA | * | |
| 1968 | The Easy Part's Over | RCA | * | |
| 1968 | Let the Chips Fall | RCA | * | |
| 1969 | Kaw-Linga | RCA | * | |
| 1969 | All I Have To Offer You (Is Me) | RCA | * | X |
| 1969 | (I'm So) Afraid of Losing You Again | RCA | * | X |
| 1970 | Is Anybody Goin' to San Antone | RCA | * | X |
| 1970 | Wonder Could I Live There Anymore | RCA | * | X |
| 1970 | I Can't Believe That You Stopped Loving Me | RCA | * | X |

* Smash Hit
X Crossover to Pop

| YEAR | SINGLE | LABEL | C&W | POP |
|------|--------|-------|-----|-----|
| 1971 | I'd Rather Love You | RCA | * | x |
| 1971 | Did You Think to Pray/Let Me Live | RCA | | |
| 1971 | I'm Just Me | RCA | * | x |
| 1971 | Kiss an Angel Good Morning | RCA | * | x |
| 1972 | All His Children (with Henry Mancini) | RCA | * | x |
| 1972 | It's Gonna Take a Little Bit Longer | RCA | * | |
| 1972 | She's Too Good To Be True | RCA | * | |
| 1973 | A Shoulder To Cry On | RCA | * | |
| 1973 | Don't Fight the Feelings Of Love | RCA | * | |
| 1973 | Amazing Love | RCA | * | |
| 1974 | We Could | RCA | * | |
| 1974 | Mississippi Cotton-Pickin' Delta Man | RCA | * | x |
| 1974 | Then Who Am I | RCA | * | |
| 1975 | I Ain't All Bad | RCA | * | |
| 1975 | Hope You're Feelin' Me (Like I'm Feelin' You) | RCA | * | |
| 1975 | The Happiness of Having You | RCA | * | |
| 1976 | My Eyes Can Only See as Far as You | RCA | * | |
| 1976 | A Whole Lotta Things To Sing About | RCA | * | |
| 1977 | She's Just an Old Love Turned Memory | RCA | * | |
| 1977 | I'll Be Leaving Alone | RCA | * | |
| 1977 | More To Me | RCA | * | |
| 1978 | Somebody Loves You Honey | RCA | * | |
| 1978 | When I Stop Leaving (I'll Be Gone) | RCA | * | |
| 1978 | Burgers and Fries | RCA | * | |
| 1979 | You're My Jamaica | RCA | * | |

| YEAR | SINGLE | LABEL | C&W | POP |
|------|--------|-------|-----|-----|
| 1979 | Dallas Cowboys | RCA | | |
| 1979 | Missin' You | RCA | | * |
| 1980 | Honky-Tonk Blues | RCA | | * |
| 1980 | You Win Again | RCA | | * |
| 1980 | You Almost Slipped My Mind/Never Been So Loved (In All My Life) | RCA | | * |
| 1981 | Mountain of Love | RCA | | * |
| 1981 | Roll On Mississippi | RCA | | * |
| 1981 | Never Been So Loved | RCA | | * |
| 1982 | I Don't Think She's In Love Anymore | RCA | | * |
| 1982 | Why Baby Why | RCA | | * |
| 1982 | You're So Good When You're Bad | RCA | | * |
| 1983 | More and More | RCA | | * |
| 1983 | Night Games | RCA | | * |
| 1983 | Ev'ry Heart Should Have One | RCA | | * |

* Smash Hit
X Crossover to Pop

**143**

Dolly Parton—talent, good looks, and charisma.

*What I'd like people to say about me in a hundred years is—*
*"Boy, she looks great for her age."*
　　*Dolly Parton, television interview with Barbara Walters*

Sometimes people aren't exactly the way they appear. Then again, sometimes they are. On her first hit record, Dolly sang: "This dumb blonde ain't nobody's fool." Indeed, she isn't. Here is what author Rita Davenport wrote in her book, *Making Time, Making Money:*

> *My friend Dolly Parton . . . started programming herself from a very early age to be successful. When she was only seven years old, the fourth in a family of twelve children, she decided she wanted to be a big star—"the biggest in the world." She wanted pretty clothes and attention and to buy things for mama and daddy. She admitted to having heartaches and disappointments, but she never let them block her vision of the future.*

People in the entertainment business respect Dolly Parton as an intelligent businesswoman who has planned and navigated her way to the top. Quite unlike the typical "dumb blondes" in the movies who are exploited by their managers and just about everyone else around them, Dolly makes it crystal clear that she is the brains behind all those dumb-blonde wigs.

"The older I get and the more business I do, the more I understand how important it is to stay in control," Dolly told *Parade* magazine. "I am a product. I own me. I will pay for advice (from lawyers and other advisors), but I will make the final decisions myself."

This shrewd and hard-headed approach to business—which Dolly calls "good ol' country horse sense" —was nurtured during her formative years growing up with her eleven brothers and sisters in a two-room shack in Tennessee's Smoky Mountains. The pain of growing up poor and hungry weighed heavily on the young girl and, like Cinderella in the fairy tale, Dolly dreamed that someone would magically turn her shack into a palace and her raggedy clothes into magnificent gowns.

Although Dolly's dream was not unique, her talents and strength of purpose were. She started writing songs at the age of seven, and her folks quickly realized that Dolly was more than just another starstruck country girl. By the time she was ten, her uncle got her a regular spot singing and playing guitar on a Knoxville radio show: This led to a debut performance at Nashville's famous Grand Ole Opry when she was twelve.

"They told me I couldn't go on because I didn't belong to a union," Dolly recalled in *Cosmopolitan* magazine. "But I saw Johnny Cash and just walked up to him and told him I had to sing. . . . He brought me out and introduced me and I brought down the house. I thought I was a star right there and then, and I was so proud because I knew my parents were listenin' to the show on the radio back home."

Dolly could have quit school to pursue her career as a child star, but she decided to wait until she graduated from high school. "I figured I'd need an education to go out in the world," she told *Cosmopolitan*. "And I knew I'd be the first member of my family in generations to leave the mountains and actually *go* out in the world. I never doubted I'd make it."

The day after high-school graduation, Dolly packed an old cardboard suitcase, kissed her family goodbye, and boarded a bus to Nashville. In typical fairy-tale style, she met her husband-to-be, Carl Dean, at a laundromat on the day she arrived in Nashville. In less than a year, Dolly had a hit record and a featured spot on the Porter Wagoner tour and television show.

Back in the late sixties, country music veteran Porter Wagoner put together a show that was considered one of the smoothest and most sophisticated in all of country music. With the addition of Dolly, Wagoner was able to successfully combine traditional folk elements with rock and pop influences to put on a show rivaled only by Johnny Cash and his troupe. However, Dolly was already looking not only beyond Porter Wagoner, but also beyond the confines of the entire Nashville scene.

Porter Wagoner's contribution to Dolly's career is undeniable, although it is only fair to point out that he enjoyed his greatest success during Dolly's six-year stint with him. Together they had over a dozen best-selling records for RCA. But Dolly was much too talented and ambitious to play second fiddle to anyone for very long. In 1974, she struck out on her own with a string of top-five hits that included "Jolene," "I Will Always Love You," "Love Is Like a Butterfly," "The Bargain Store," "The Seeker," "We Used To," and "All I Can Do." In 1975 and 1976, Dolly won the Country Music Association award for the best Female Singer of the Year. During this period, Dolly formed her own band—Dolly Parton's Traveling Family Band — got her own syndicated TV show, and had her songs recorded by such stars as Linda Ronstadt, Olivia Newton-John, and Emmylou Harris.

This might have been enough success for some people, but not for Dolly Parton. "I had a following and I was famous," Dolly told *Parade* magazine, "but I wasn't really sellin' that many records — 100,000, 200,000 was the biggest thing I ever had. It was like beatin' your head against a wall. After a while I got to thinkin' there was a need for a change."

We are more accustomed now to seeing established country singers crossover into pop. But in the mid-seventies, it was a risky move. Dolly understood that there was the potential of selling millions of records with a pop hit, but she had no assurance that an unfamiliar audience would accept her. At the same time, she risked losing the country audience she had spent years building up. All this didn't faze Dolly in the least. She believed that she had something unique to offer listeners outside of the country field. And if she needed to change some things about the direction of her music, she felt she could do this without compromise. As she was fond of saying at the time, "I'm not leavin' country, I'm just takin' it with me."

Dolly fired her band and signed on with the high-powered, Los Angeles-based management company, Katz–Gallin–Morey. The albums that followed this move—*Here You Come Again, Heartbreaker, Great Balls of Fire, Best of Dolly Parton,* and *Heartbreak Express*—all made over one million dollars in total record sales. Suddenly, this poor little girl from the Smoky Mountains with the down-home, folksy voice was an international star who traded witty lines with Johnny Carson on the "Tonight" show and was featured on the cover of dozens of magazines.

Making the jump from country star to pop star was not so difficult for Dolly. Singing in the studio, performing on stage, and even writing songs are pretty much the same in both fields. Mostly, it's the musical arrangements and the size of the royalty checks that are different. Dolly wanted the increased fame and riches that becoming a national star would bring, but she also welcomed the challenge of expanding her musical horizons.

Dolly's vocal and songwriting talents encompass several musical styles. Her voice has a down-to-earth quality that reflects her childhood years in the Smoky Mountains. But like the late Elvis Presley, Dolly is as at home with a Las Vegas audience as she is on the stage of Nashville's Grand Ole Opry. Her unique style makes her one of those performers whose personality comes across strong and true, no matter what the musical accompaniment. Perhaps that is why she was the first female recording artist to reach the top of the pop, country, and contemporary charts (with her self-penned single "9 to 5").

In her typical fashion, Dolly often jokes about not being a particularly good singer. But, in fact, she is one of our best and most important contemporary female vocalists. Although she is often imitated, Dolly has an unmistakable quality in her voice that somehow combines elements of traditional American folk music, the strength and power of religious music, and her own unique brand of fun.

Original vocal talents are rare enough in popular music. But when that talent is combined with the ability to write great songs, it's a combination that is hard to beat. Dolly's songwriting skills have helped her become an awesome force in the music business. Noted song publisher and executive producer Charles Koppelman, who worked with Dolly on several of her biggest albums, describes the talent to consistently write memorable songs as "the most essential part of making hit records." Perhaps that is why Dolly has gained so much attention and respect from her peers in the music business.

As with her singing, Dolly's songwriting covers a wide range of emotional territory. In songs like "Coat of Many Colors" and "Me and Little Andy," Dolly reveals the pain and loneliness she experienced as a young girl. In one song, "Jeannie's Afraid of the Dark," Dolly tells the story of how one of her classmates once locked her up in a dark closet at school. A number of Dolly's other hit tunes are good-time clap-alongs like, "Two Doors Down." Others, like "Blue Ridge Mountain Boy" and "Down From Dover," show her great skill at developing characters and exploring serious subjects within the confines of a popular song.

As the first country-and-western female star to have a major impact on the pop market, Dolly has secured a position as an important figure in the evolution of American popular music. As much as anyone, Dolly has extended the connections between folk traditions and contemporary styles. At times, she writes and sings about the wonderment of nature, as in

"Early Morning Breeze." At other times, she writes with great insight about love relationships.

"My mistakes are no worse than yours just because I'm a woman," Dolly writes in "Just Because I'm a Woman." And though she doesn't consider herself a spokesperson for women's lib, Dolly explores the subject of love in ways that are unusual and daring for a female country singer. In fact, one of her songs, "The Bargain Store," was explicit and straightforward enough to get banned from many country radio stations.

It should come as no great surprise that Dolly's talent, looks, and personal charisma were just too strong to be limited to singing and songwriting. It was only a matter of time until she made the jump to movies. She might not be the first country star to appear on the big screen, but she certainly has made the biggest splash. Reviewers and other movie people have compared Dolly to Mae West and Marilyn Monroe, as a sex symbol with a natural flair for comic acting. As Colin Higgins, who directed Dolly in her first movie, *9 to 5,* told *Cosmopolitan*: "Dolly Parton has the kind of on-screen charisma that demands attention. She's bigger than life, warm and vital. I predict she's going to be one of the superstars of the movies."

What's left for Dolly now that she has seemingly achieved her major goals? Every detail of her Cinderella story seems in place. She became a big country

Dolly with actress Goldie Hawn—now she's a movie star in her own right.

music star, emerged as the first woman in her field to have a gold pop album, and received instant stardom in her first movie role, holding her own with co-stars Jane Fonda and Lily Tomlin. What more is there for her to accomplish?

"Everybody has their own purpose in life and I'm just trying to fulfill what I think mine is," Dolly told ABC–TV's Barbara Walters. "I'd like to start a city called Dollywood U.S.A.—something like Disneyland but in the mountains. . . . I'd also like to start a line of clothes and cosmetics for the kind of people who would come to my concerts."

In the coming years, Dolly probably will dabble in these projects. For the present, though, she plans to write songs, travel with her band, and continue with her movie career. But there are a few things Dolly feels she needs to solve before she feels completely happy with herself.

Many people use gimmicks to launch their careers in show business. But when your gimmick involves making people think you're a joke, it can present a special set of problems. The Dolly Parton look emphasizes the word *big*. Although she is only five feet tall, her puffed-up blonde wigs, and her waistline and bustline make her look something like a caricature of a dumb, blonde floozy. This is a gimmick which Dolly plays to the hilt. But in another sense, it is a very real part of who she is.

"What they used to call 'cheap trash' in our town is what I wanted to look like," Dolly told Barbara Walters, "because I liked the clothes, I liked the hair, and I liked the flair. . . . See, my idea of beauty came from *True Confessions* magazine and the floozies in our town. . . . That's how I wanted to be."

Dolly believes that she has reached a point in her career where she could be accepted without playing the floozy in her looks. In spite of the jokes she makes about herself being ugly and fat, she is actually a very attractive woman who no longer needs gimmicks. She herself admits that she could get away with less, but laughingly confesses that she'd rather have more. At the same time, she wants the public to know that she is not a joke, but a highly intelligent person who is serious about her work and her personal life.

The best moments of Dolly's personal life are spent with her husband Carl at an eighty-acre estate outside of Nashville called Tara. "The place is for Carl and me," Dolly told *Cosmopolitan.* "We lock the gate and turn off the phones. . . . I'm gone so much, we need that time together."

Two rooms in the house are filled with Dolly's clothes, 350 wigs, and 2,000 pairs of shoes—all slated for a museum that she plans to build someday. The rest of the house is a sanctuary for the privacy that Dolly needs and Carl demands. As far as anyone can tell, Carl has never been photographed or interviewed, and some rumors have even surfaced that he doesn't exist. But Dolly explains her husband's avoidance of the press by pointing out that he wouldn't want people coming over to him when he goes to the store and asking, "Don't I know you?"

In a way, Carl seems to represent Dolly's other side —a side that fans rarely get to see, but one that she would like everyone to know exists. In an age where well-known personalities are afraid to go out in public without bodyguards, it is important for fans to understand that no matter what kinds of clothes and makeup performers wear to win their audiences, they are human beings with the same needs as the rest of us. In spite of her extremely high visibility, Dolly does not hide from her public.

"I still have fun meeting people," she told *Us* magazine. "I have a lot of sisters and friends who are the same size and who could buy [my clothes] for me, but I just like to get out (and go shopping)."

It is interesting to note that the same performers who have satisfying and "normal" relationships at home often have an easier time meeting and touching the public than those who are isolated and troubled in their private lives. Perhaps that is one reason why Dolly Parton was able to bounce back so quickly from an illness that caused her to faint while performing during the summer of 1982 and landed her in the hospital. While the gossip magazines went wild with all kinds of stories, Dolly took four months off and rested in the peace and quiet of Tara. Dolly made a complete recovery from her physical problems and continued pretty much as before. We will be hearing and seeing much more of Dolly in the future. And while not all of her singing, moviemaking, and other activities will please all fans and critics, Dolly fully intends to pursue any project she feels comfortable with.

So there we have it. The Dolly Parton story, a study in contradictions. The puffed-up, painted floozy with the big brain. The country gal rooted in the natural beauty and dark emotions of mountain folk music who conquered the entire world with her commercial sound. The faithful, loving wife who freely admits that she is a flirt. And the hard-nosed businesswoman who is so friendly and open, she makes you want to hug her. It all just goes to show that people aren't always the way they appear. Then again, sometimes they are.

# Dolly Parton Collector's Guide

| YEAR | ALBUM | LABEL |
|------|-------|-------|
| 1968 | Just Because I'm a Woman | RCA Victor |
| 1969 | In the Good Old Days | RCA Victor |
| 1969 | My Blue Ridge Mountain Boy | RCA Victor |
| 1970 | Fairest of Them All | RCA Victor |
| 1970 | A Real Live Dolly | RCA Victor |
| 1970 | Hello I'm Dolly | Monument |
| 1970 | Best of Dolly Parton | RCA Victor |
| 1971 | Golden Streets of Glory | RCA Victor |
| 1971 | Joshua | RCA Victor |
| 1971 | As Long as I Have Love | Monument |
| 1971 | Coat of Many Colors | RCA Victor |
| 1972 | Touch Your Woman | RCA Victor |
| 1972 | My Favorite Songwriter: Porter Wagoner | RCA |
| 1973 | Just the Way I Am | Camden |
| 1973 | My Tennessee Mountain Home | RCA |
| 1973 | Mine | RCA |
| 1974 | Real Live Bubbling Over | RCA |
| 1974 | Love Is Like a Butterfly | RCA |
| 1975 | Best of Dolly Parton | RCA |
| 1976 | All I Can Do | RCA |
| 1977 | New Harvest . . . First Gathering | RCA |
| 1977 | Here You Come Again | RCA |
| 1978 | Heartbreaker | RCA |
| 1979 | Great Balls of Fire | RCA |
| 1980 | Dolly Dolly Dolly | RCA |
| 1980 | 9 to 5 and Odd Jobs | RCA |
| 1982 | Heartbreak Express | RCA |
| 1982 | The Best Little Whorehouse in Texas (motion picture soundtrack) | RCA |

**159**

| YEAR | ALBUM | LABEL |
|---|---|---|
| 1982 | Kris, Willie, Dolly, and Brenda . . . The Winning Hand (with Kris Kristofferson, Willie Nelson and Brenda Lee) | Monument |
| 1983 | Burlap and Satin | RCA |

| YEAR | SINGLE | LABEL | C&W | POP |
|---|---|---|---|---|
| 1967 | Dumb Blonde | Monument | | |
| 1967 | Something Fishy | Monument | | |
| 1968 | Just Because I'm a Woman | RCA | | |
| 1968 | In the Good Old Days (When Times Were Bad) | RCA | | |
| 1969 | Daddy | RCA | | |
| 1969 | In the Ghetto | RCA | | |
| 1969 | My Blue Ridge Mountain Boy | RCA | | |
| 1970 | Daddy Come and Get Me | RCA | | |
| 1970 | Mule Skinner Blues | RCA | * | |
| 1970 | Joshua | RCA | * | |
| 1971 | Comin' For to Carry Me Home | RCA | | |
| 1971 | My Blue Tears | RCA | | |
| 1971 | Coat of Many Colors | RCA | * | |
| 1972 | Touch Your Woman | RCA | * | |
| 1972 | Washday Blues | RCA | | |
| 1973 | My Tennessee Mountain Home | RCA | | |
| 1973 | Travelin' Man | RCA | | |
| 1973 | Jolene | RCA | * | x |
| 1974 | I Will Always Love You | RCA | * | |
| 1974 | Love Is Like a Butterfly | RCA | * | |
| 1975 | The Bargain Store | RCA | * | |
| 1975 | The Seeker | RCA | * | |

| YEAR | SINGLE | LABEL | C&W | POP |
|------|--------|-------|-----|-----|
| 1975 | We Used To | RCA | * | |
| 1976 | Hey Lucky Lady | RCA | | |
| 1976 | All I Can Do | RCA | * | |
| 1977 | Light of a Clear Blue Morning | RCA | * | x |
| 1977 | Here You Come Again | RCA | * | x |
| 1978 | It's All Wrong, But It's All Right/ Two Doors Down | RCA | * | x |
| 1978 | Heartbreaker | RCA | * | x |
| 1978 | I Really Got the Feeling/Baby I'm Burning | RCA | * | x |
| 1979 | You're the Only One | RCA | * | |
| 1979 | Sweet Summer Lovin'/Great Balls of Fire | RCA | * | |
| 1980 | Starting Over Again | RCA | * | |
| 1980 | Making Plans | RCA | * | |
| 1980 | Old Flames Can't Hold a Candle To You | RCA | * | |
| 1980 | If You Go I'll Follow You (with Porter Wagoner) | RCA | | |
| 1980 | 9 to 5 | RCA | * | x |
| 1981 | House of the Rising Sun | RCA | | |
| 1981 | But You Know I Love You | RCA | * | |
| 1982 | Single Woman | RCA | * | |
| 1982 | Heartbreak Express | RCA | * | |
| 1982 | I Will Always Love You/Do I Ever Cross Your Mind | RCA | * | x |
| 1982 | Hard Candy Christmas | RCA | * | |
| 1982 | Everything's Beautiful (In It's Own Way) (with Willie Nelson) | RCA | * | |
| 1983 | Potential New Boyfriend | RCA | * | |
| 1983 | Islands in the Stream | RCA | * | x |

* Smash Hit
X Crossover to Pop

Kenny Rogers—talent plus brains.

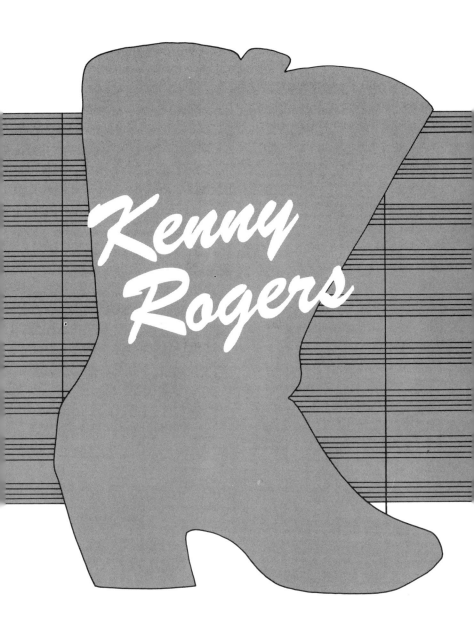

*I think a smart man isn't necessarily the one who knows all the answers, but knows where to find them.*

*Kenny Rogers,* Record World

Most superstars in any field get where they are because they have something unique to offer. In country music, we can point to the personalities and voices of people like Willie Nelson, Dolly Parton, and Johnny Cash to explain why they are so popular.

Kenny Rogers's most outstanding quality, however, might be that there is no one thing about him that really stands out. He's got a very nice voice, but certainly not one you would call unique. He's a pleasant-looking man, but again, you'd probably have trouble picking him out in a crowd. Yet Kenny Rogers recently signed a new record contract for a reported $20 million—perhaps the largest figure ever given to a recording artist. RCA, Kenny's record label, has no doubt that his record sales will more than justify their giant investment. Most music industry experts agree with them. What is it then that makes Kenny Rogers one of the most successful performers in the world?

"I don't consider myself a good musician . . . or . . . a great singer," Kenny told *Record Magazine World.* "Basically, I'm . . . an entertainer. . . . I go out (on stage to) make people laugh some, sing along some, and have a good time. . . . What I hope for my hour on the stage is not that (people say) he's a great singer, a great musician, but just that it was fun."

If providing audiences with a good time is Kenny's stock in trade, he must be doing an awfully good job. You don't have seven platinum (million-selling) albums in a row, over a dozen top-ten singles, starring roles in at least three films, and numerous prime-time television specials without making a lot of people happy.

There are many flashes in the pan in popular music, people who have a hit record or two and then disappear from the spotlight. But Kenny Rogers, who had his first hit as a teenager, worked hard and kept at it for twenty years before reaching true superstardom. In that time, he played in jazz combos, folk-singing groups, and rock bands. Better musicians with better voices took their bow in the spotlight and faded from glory as the musical trend they were part of was replaced by something new. But Kenny kept growing and changing with the times until he finally carved out a permanent spot as a superstar.

## Not an Overnight Success Story

Kenny Rogers was born in 1938 in Houston, Texas. His father Edward worked a variety of manual labor jobs to put food on the table for his wife Lucille and their eight children. Like so many others in that part of the world, the Rogers family would spend Sunday afternoons with friends pickin' and singin' country and gospel tunes. Kenny loved those gatherings, as he had a natural feel and ear for music. He soon made the connection between performing music and the chance to rise above the relative poverty and struggles that marked his family's existence. By the time he was sixteen, Kenny had saved enough money from working as a busboy to buy his own guitar. Together with a few friends, Kenny formed his first group, the Scholars. Like most high-school bands, the fellows hoped to win a few talent contests, make a few extra dollars, and attract girls.

Even at that very early stage, Kenny had an inkling that better things might be coming his way. His brother Lelan, who worked for a local record distributor, arranged for the Scholars to record the tunes of a local songwriter. A few of the songs became regional hits in Houston, and the recording career of a future country music superstar had taken its first giant step.

Shortly before his abbreviated college career, Kenny recorded some songs by Ray Dogget, a Houston disc jockey, and one of them, "That Crazy Feeling," actually became a million-selling hit. Kenny appeared on Dick Clark's "American Bandstand," which was, at that time, the hottest music show on television. But it was 1957, and in those days you didn't make a lot of money from one hit record. Most of the singers who made a splash during that era were "one-hit wonders" who were never heard from again.

Although Kenny was eventually to collect hit records like some people collect stamps or coins, he was not prepared to capitalize on his first million-selling record. Aside from not having a developed stage act to mount any kind of a live tour, Kenny also lacked a good song to record on the heels of his first success.

Kenny's folks had other ideas about Kenny's involvement with music. They had no desire for their son to become a professional musician, and they encouraged him to go to college and study to become an architect. Disappointed and uncertain about the future, Kenny decided to give college a try. He didn't finish his first term. His brief academic life was accompanied by a stint as a backup bass player for a female guitarist for eighteen dollars a night. Shortly after leaving college, Kenny hooked up with a blind piano player named Bobby Doyle and became part of one of Houston's most successful club acts. During his tenure with the Bobby Doyle Trio, Kenny got to meet stars like Tony Bennett and Liza Minnelli. One popular star of that era, Kirby Stone, liked the group so much that he hired them to accompany him on a national tour. Kenny credits Stone with teaching him to become a great showman, but Kirby feels that showmanship was something Kenny came by quite naturally.

"The thing about him that was more interesting than anything else," Stone recalls, "is that he was an absolute professional on stage from he day he started working with me. . . . If he had any personal problems, he left them off stage. . . . He's one of the easiest people I've worked with in the business. . . . He was and is a pro."

Through Kirby Stone, the Bobby Doyle Trio landed a recording contract with Columbia Records. The album they made, *In a Most Unusual Way,* was an artistic success but a commercial failure. In 1965, after playing together for six years, the group disbanded. There is no denying that the experience Kenny gained as part of the trio helped make him a better musician.

"I worked his butt off," Bobby Doyle told *Record World.* "Rehearsing as well as performing gigs, six mornings, afternoons, and nights for over six years. That's what I call discipline. . . . If I made any big contribution to Kenny's career, it was the constant work and learning of tunes."

After the trio broke up, Kenny continued to play a similar kind of pop-jazz with a group called the Lively

Ones. In 1966, toward the tail end of the folk music craze, Kirby Stone's managers remembered Kenny when they started putting together a touring version of the New Christy Minstrels. The group had already had hits like, "Green Green" and "This Land Is Your Land." But at the point Kenny became involved, they were mostly a live act living off their previous hits.

For a while, Kenny considered remaining in Houston. He was making a good living working local clubs. Besides, he had a wife, a daughter, and a house in the suburbs. Yet, Kenny felt that the chance to appear with a nationally recognized group would constitute a step up in his career. So, against the wishes of his soon-to-be-divorced first wife, Kenny hit the road.

Former New Christy Minstrel member Terry Williams recalls how Kenny became part of that group:

> The Christies were looking for a bassist who also sang tenor, and I remember them calling Kenny. They had him audition over the phone. At the time, he was in a very strange position, in some hallway or something. They kept asking him to sing louder and louder, and he was trying to sing with all these people around him, all staring at him while he sang into the phone.

By the time Kenny joined the New Christy Minstrels, the folk music trend that had spawned the group had taken on a stronger beat and added the resonance of electric guitars. What had started out as a bland rendering of old traditional American favorites by pretty young boys and girls had now been taken over by long-haired American rock and rollers like Bob Dylan and the Byrds, and Englishmen like the Beatles, the Animals, and the Rolling Stones. The Minstrels were making a nice living playing the safe kind of folk music that much of middle America still wanted to hear. But Kenny and some of his cohorts wanted to become part of the more exciting and potentially more rewarding new folk rock.

One of the Minstrels, Mike Settle, had written some tunes that reflected the influences of both rock and folk music. He asked Kenny and fellow Minstrels Terry Williams and Thelma Camacho to help him work up some of these songs. When they asked the group's managers if some of the new material could be included in the act, they were told that it wasn't wise to tamper with a proven, money-making formula. The four singers then decided to leave the Minstrels and form a new group, the First Edition.

The year was 1967, and Kenny Rogers was about to begin another phase of his career. The First Edition decided that they wanted to shed the clean-cut look they had as New Christy Minstrels and adopt the long-haired, psychedelic image that most rock bands featured in those days. Kenny—as the oldest member of the group—seemed the least likely candidate for a psychedelic-looking rock band. With his jazz and supper club background, he was the last to be accepted as a member of the First Edition. But Kenny had the kind of voice that was needed, as well as a willingness to change his image to fit the situation. Terry Williams, another original member of the group, remembers how it all began:

> There weren't many groups in '67 who sang really well, so we decided to take a shot at it. . . . We worked up a few numbers while playing at a little hotel on the Sunset Strip called the Sands. It's hard to think back on it, because it all happened so quickly—it was like a dream. We got together in 1967, and six months later, we had a number-two record, "Just Dropped In (To See What Condition My Condition Was In)." It was incredible.

Nineteen sixty-eight was a banner year for the First Edition. They were constantly touring, appearing on television, and holding interviews with the press. However, the follow-up records to "Just Dropped In" were just not selling. It wasn't until 1969 that the First Edition had their next big hit, "But You Know I Love You." As with "Just Dropped In," the song was written by Mike Settle and featured Kenny singing lead. The plan was to follow "But You Know I Love You" with a similar tune. But another song—"Ruby, Don't Take

Your Love To Town" — was receiving such tremendous response that the group's management decided to release it under the name of Kenny Rogers and the First Edition. Although the group was originally conceived as a partnership with everyone making an equal contribution, it was necessary to continue using Kenny's name in front of the First Edition since the record label feared that listeners might think that he was no longer with the group. Kenny's long-time manager Ken Kragen explains how Kenny's role in the group evolved:

*Kenny wasn't the leader in (the early) days; Mike Settle was. But it was Kenny's voice on hits like "Reuben James," "Ruby," and so on. We reached a point about three or four years into it when we had one record out as Kenny Rogers and the First Edition and one just as the First Edition; at that point, I began to think it was a lot easier to market a group if people had one name to identify with. So, I sold the group (having Kenny's name up front). It created some problems, frankly, but in the long run, it was the right move. Kenny was also the most aggressive businessman, despite his laid-back nature. He had the most drive, and people kind of gravitated towards him.*

After a number of hit records, the First Edition hit a slump in the mid-seventies, and Kragen had to come up with creative ways to generate work for the group. "We found other avenues," he recalls. "We played Las Vegas regularly. . . . There was the 'Roll-in' TV series out of Canada, which was eventually syndicated in 192 markets. I also found a way to get into the (state) fair business. Finally, there was New Zealand, where the group played 57 sell-out concerts on three different tours over . . . a three-year period."

In spite of Kragen's efforts, the First Edition disbanded in 1976, and Kenny launched a new solo career. There was rough going at first, as Ken Kragen recalls:

*Kenny usually doesn't get depressed—he's usually on a pretty even keel. But he was as low as I've ever seen him then. He even wanted to quit. . . . Kenny's band wasn't very good at first, (and) he wasn't used to being an opening act. . . . It was really the depths.*

Kenny's career soon took a permanent turn for the better. In 1977, he had four top-ten country hits: "Love Lifted Me," "Homemade Love," "While the Feeling's Good," and "Laura." In June another one of his country hits, "Lucille," became a top-five pop hit, and Kenny's star really began to rise. That year, he won a grammy and two Country Music Association awards for "Lucille." This might have been a lofty goal for some entertainers, but for Kenny Rogers and his manager Ken Kragen, it was only the beginning.

"It's a lot easier to push hard once you've got a career going than to get it started," Kragen told *Record World* in 1978. "That means that while Kenny's exploding, I'm working doubly hard. This is the time to put the money and effort into Kenny that will move him from a one-million to a five-million seller."

Kenny's record company, United Artists, also felt that the time was right to get behind his career 110 percent. "When 'Lucille' broke big," recalls former United Artists executive Artie Mogull, "we launched one of the most extensive image-building campaigns on Kenny in the history of the record business. We spent a substantial amount of money, but it was worth every penny because Kenny has fantastic instincts for the record business. He is the most cooperative, hardest-working artist I've ever met."

Everyone who has ever been associated with Kenny Rogers mentions his outstanding business ability. This is somewhat unusual for music superstars. With a few notable exceptions, most highly successful entertainers leave their business affairs to other people to handle.

"I think [my skill as a businessman] has been my real strength," Kenny recently told *Country Rhythms* magazine. "I'm real business-oriented. I absolutely love negotiating, I negotiate my own contracts. . . . If

I make mistakes, I live by them. . . . But I've been fortunate that I haven't made that many mistakes that have hurt my career."

Kenny Rogers is an exceptional businessman who had the patience to wait twenty years before making it to the top. But this is not enough to explain the man's appeal as a performer, recording artist, and screen personality. People have long debated the question of whether the public will buy anything if it is put in front of them long enough. While it is true that more than a few talented recording artists never had a hit record because their record company did not get behind them, it is also true that people won't spend their hard-earned money on a record or a concert ticket unless they are being entertained. And if there's one thing Kenny Rogers understands even better than business, it's how to make records and give concerts that make people feel good.

Larry Butler, who has produced many of Kenny's hit records, feels that audiences respond to the overall quality and sincerity of Kenny's work:

*We're not thinking about a particular audience when we're in the studio. We're thinking about people listening to the records. . . . We're trying to cut a good record. I've cut records that I thought would cross over (from country hits to national pop hits) that didn't. I've cut records that I knew there was no way in the world they would, and they did. So I've given up on trying to figure out what's going to cross over and what's going to do what. . . . But Kenny's a very versatile artist. He appeals to a lot of different types of people—attorneys, doctors, housewives, farmers, bricklayers, TV repairmen. . . . We try to entertain everybody.*

Kenny's approach to live performing is just as well rounded and personal as his records. He has been called the "Mick Jagger of middle America" and a "symbol of goodness and decency in a cold, scary world." Yet Kenny seems remarkably unimpressed by all these labels. When he talks about performing, it is with the same kind of levelheaded approach that characterizes everything he does. In an interview with *Record World* magazine, he said:

*It has always been my contention that music falls into the same category as any kind of show, and that it should serve two purposes. Not only should it make me happy, but it should entertain the people listening. . . . If either one of us isn't having a good time, then it isn't serving its purpose. . . . I think if a person comes on the stage and entertains only himself, and he and the band laugh at each other and have a great time when the people don't know what's . . . going on, then he's defeated his purpose for being there. And that is, number one, to fulfill that need that someone felt badly enough to pay (twelve or fifteen) bucks for a ticket: they didn't come out to see you entertain yourself, they came out to be entertained and enjoy what*

*they can't catch in a record, which is that live, personal per-*
*formance.*

Perhaps it is Kenny's ability to understand his audience that helps make him so successful at what he
does. Unlike some artists who insist on recording only
songs that they write themselves, Kenny picks the best
songs he can find. He told *Country Rhythms* magazine:

> *I like songs that touch basic emotions. I think all of us suffer
> from the same problems. We all have insecurities. We all fear
> rejection and none of us want to be old and alone. I think if you
> can touch on some of those things, then you transcend the musi-
> cal form that it started from. . . . I look for songs that tell a story
> (and) also that make you care about the person involved.*

Kenny's songs tell such powerful stories that two of
them, "The Gambler" and "Coward of the County",
have been transformed into highly successful TV
movies with Kenny as their star. In fact, the people he
portrays and projects in his songs have become more
notorious than Kenny himself. For a man who has
been in the business so long and who is working on his
third marriage, his personal life has been remarkably
free of the kinds of rumors and scandals that thrive
around many superstars. Maybe that's why the press
made such a big fuss when Kenny and his wife
Marianne bought a $14.5 million house in California.

**177**

"I don't have any controversy about me," he told columnist Lisa Robinson.

*I'm happily married, I don't go out and carouse. I'm not into doing drugs. So they pick on the two obvious things: that I'm happily married and that I've made a lot of money. I don't know what else they could write about me that would be sensational enough to demand people to pay attention. . . . Six years ago, Marianne and I were trying to decide if we could move from a $220-a-month apartment to a $300-a-month apartment. So as far as I'm concerned, this is the American success story.*

It's hard to imagine how much further Kenny Rogers can take this amazing success story. Between 1978–82, he had four multimillion-selling albums— *The Gambler, Greatest Hits, Share Your Love With Me,* and *Love Will Turn You Around.* During that time, he changed from being a moderately successful recording artist and entertainer to one who signed a record contract that reportedly outdistanced those signed by superstars like Diana Ross, Paul McCartney, and the Rolling Stones.

Yet Kenny Rogers doesn't fit the stereotype of the greedy, high-rolling pop star. He is deeply involved in a number of worthy causes, most notably, a movement to end world hunger and the Special Olympics. He has also helped launch two other successful careers —those of singers Dottie West and Kim Carnes. He also finds time for his loving wife, of whom he says:

"Marianne helped me realize that success is not the most important thing in the world; having someone to share your ups and downs with *is*."

Now that Kenny has found such a great measure of personal happiness and material success, there's no telling what he will do next. But with his acute business sense and his almost uncanny feel for what all kinds of audiences enjoy listening to, we can be certain that we'll be hearing and seeing a lot more of him in the years to come.

Kenny with Sheena Easton.

# Kenny Rogers Collector's Guide

| YEAR | ALBUM | LABEL |
|------|-------|-------|
| 1959 | One Dozen Goldies | Carlton |
| 968 | First Edition | Reprise |
| 1968 | First Edition's Second | Reprise |
| 1969 | First Edition '69 | Reprise |
| 1969 | Ruby Don't Take Your Love to Town (with the First Edition) | Reprise |
| 1970 | Something's Burning (with the First Edition) | Reprise |
| 1970 | Tell It All Brother (with the First Edition) | Reprise |
| 1971 | Fools (soundtrack) (with the First Edition) | Reprise |
| 1971 | Kenny Rogers and the First Edition's Greatest Hits | Reprise |
| 1971 | Transitions (with the First Edition) | Reprise |
| 1972 | The Ballad of Callico (with the First Edition) | Reprise |
| 1972 | Back Roads (with the First Edition) | Jolly Rogers |
| 1973 | Monumental (with the First Edition) | Jolly Rogers |
| 1973 | Rollin' (with the First Edition) | Jolly Rogers |
| 1976 | Love Lifted Me | U.A. |
| 1977 | Kenny Rogers/Lucille | U.A. |
| 1977 | Daytime Friends | U.A. |
| 1977 | Ten Years of Gold | U.A. |
| 1978 | Every Time Two Fools Collide (with Dottie West) | U.A. |
| 1978 | Love or Something Like It | U.A. |
| 1978 | Convoy (soundtrack) | U.A. |
| 1978 | The Gambler | U.A. |
| 1979 | Classics (with Dottie West) | U.A. |
| 1979 | Kenny | U.A. |

| YEAR | ALBUM | LABEL |
|---|---|---|
| 1979 | Kenny Rogers and the First Edition | Lakeshore Music (Warner Brothers) |
| 1980 | Kenny Rogers's Greatest Hits | Liberty |
| 1981 | Share Your Love | Liberty |
| 1982 | Kenny Rogers Christmas | Liberty |
| 1982 | Love Will Turn You Around | Liberty |
| 1983 | We've Got Tonight | Liberty |
| 1983 | Eyes That See in the Dark | RCA |

| YEAR | SINGLE | LABEL | C&W | POP |
|---|---|---|---|---|
| 1958 | That Crazy Feeling | Carlton | | |
| 1958 | For You Alone | Carlton | | |
| 1966 | Here's That Rainy Day | Mercury | | |
| 1967 | I Found a Reason (with the First Edition) | Reprise | | |
| 1968 | Just Dropped In (with the First Edition) | Reprise | | * |
| 1968 | Dream On (with the First Edition) | Reprise | | |
| 1968 | Look Around I'll Be There (with the First Edition) | Reprise | | |
| 1969 | But You Know I Love You (with the First Edition) | Reprise | | |
| 1969 | Ruby (Don't Take Your Love To Town) (with the First Edition) | Reprise | x | * |
| 1969 | Reuben James (with the First Edition) | Reprise | x | |
| 1970 | Something's Burning (with the First Edition) | Reprise | | |

* Smash Hit
X Crossover to Pop

| YEAR | SINGLE | LABEL | C&W | POP |
|------|--------|-------|-----|-----|
| 1970 | Tell It All Brother (with the First Edition) | Reprise | | |
| 1970 | Heed the Call (with the First Edition) | Reprise | | |
| 1971 | Someone Who Cares (with the First Edition) | Reprise | | |
| 1971 | Take My Hand (with the First Edition) | Reprise | | |
| 1971 | Where Does Rosie Go (with the First Edition) | Reprise | | |
| 1972 | School Teacher (with the First Edition) | Reprise | | |
| 1972 | Lady Play Your Symphony (with the First Edition) | Jolly Rogers | | |
| 1972 | Do You Remember the First Time (with the First Edition) | Jolly Rogers | | |
| 1972 | Today I Started Loving You Again (with the First Edition) | Jolly Rogers | | |
| 1973 | Lena Lookie (with the First Edition) | Jolly Rogers | | |
| 1973 | What She's Gonna Do (with the First Edition) | Jolly Rogers | | |
| 1973 | Making Music For Money (with the First Edition) | Jolly Rogers | | |
| 1975 | Love Lifted Me | U.A. | | |
| 1975 | A Homemade Love | U.A. | | |
| 1976 | While The Feeling's Good | U.A. | | |
| 1976 | Laura (What's He Got That I Ain't Got) | U.A. | | |
| 1977 | Lucille | U.A. | * | x* |
| 1977 | Daytime Friends | U.A. | * | x |
| 1977 | Sweet Music Man | U.A. | * | x |
| 1978 | Every Time Two Fools Collide (with Dottie West) | U.A. | | |

| YEAR | SINGLE | LABEL | C&W | POP |
|------|--------|-------|-----|-----|
| 1978 | Love or Something Like It | U.A. | * | |
| 1978 | Anyone Who Isn't Me Tonight (with Dottie West) | U.A. | | |
| 1978 | The Gambler | U.A. | * | |
| 1979 | She Believes In Me | U.A. | * | X |
| 1979 | All I Ever Need Is You (with Dottie West) | U.A. | * | |
| 1979 | Till I Can Make It On My Own (with Dottie West) | U.A. | * | |
| 1979 | You Decorated My Life | U.A. | * | |
| 1979 | Coward of the County | U.A. | * | |
| 1980 | Don't Fall In Love With a Dreamer (with Kim Carnes) | U.A. | * | X |
| 1980 | Love the World Away | U.A. | * | |
| 1980 | Lady | Liberty | * | X |
| 1981 | What Are We Doing In Love (with Dottie West) | Liberty | * | |
| 1981 | Share Your Love With Me | Liberty | * | |
| 1981 | I Don't Need You | Liberty | * | X |
| 1981 | Blaze of Glory | Liberty | * | |
| 1981 | Through the Years | Liberty | * | X |
| 1982 | Love Will Turn You Around | Liberty | * | X |
| 1982 | A Love Song | Liberty | * | X |
| 1983 | We've Got Tonight (with Sheena Easton) | Liberty | * | X* |
| 1983 | All My Life | Liberty | * | X |
| 1983 | Scarlet Fever | Liberty | * | |
| 1983 | Islands in the Stream (with Dolly Parton) | RCA | * | X |

* Smash Hit
X Crossover to Country

Jerry Lee Lewis—also known as "the killer."

At one time, American popular music was divided into neat little packages. There was hillbilly music for southern white folks, blues (or "race" music) for black folks, and pop music for everyone else. These distinctions still exist to some extent today, but the boundaries have become quite vague. In New York City, you can turn on one of several country radio stations and hear music that would have greatly confused listeners a few short years ago. Actually, the very thought of an all-country music radio station in a large northeastern city like New York would have seemed ridiculous back then. But times have changed. During a recent fifteen-minute segment of a country music station, the DJ played a Dolly Parton song that sounded exactly like a sixties rhythm and blues tune, a Crystal Gayle remake of a jazzy-pop ballad, a rendering of a traditional country lament by blues great B. B. King, and a popular crossover hit by rock singer Bob Seeger. Yes, indeed, times have certainly changed.

Back in Ferriday, Louisiana—where Jerry Lee Lewis was born in 1935—people knew the difference between one kind of music and another. But young

Jerry Lee grew up loving it all. Around the time that Jerry Lee was eleven, his father installed electricity in the family's rural farmhouse and purchased a radio. On Saturday nights, the Lewises would gather round to listen to broadcasts of the Grand Ole Opry and the Louisiana Hayride. Jerry Lee loved country music, especially the records of Jimmy Rodgers. However, the youngster did a lot more listening on his own. With one turn of the dial, he could tune in the big dance bands of that era. With another, he could lose himself in the raw blues of the Mississippi Delta. If he had grown up in another part of the country, Jerry Lee may have never been exposed to so many different styles of music. But he was raised in an area that has since become famous for being the most fertile meeting ground for American music.

Jerry Lee also received a great many of his musical lessons at the Assembly of God church his family attended. Unlike the restrained atmosphere of some other sects, the worshipers at Assembly of God sermons threw themselves body and soul into the music of the hymns they were singing. When the service reached a fever pitch, you could actually feel the church rocking from the collective rhythm of the congregation. Sometimes a worshiper would "get the spirit" and start twitching and dancing uncontrollably. This atmosphere was similar to the reelin' and rockin' that marked the services in black churches.

There happened to be an old piano at the Assembly of God church, and the preacher encouraged Jerry Lee to practice on it when the church was not in use. Jerry Lee was also invited to play the piano that sat in the living room of his Uncle Lee's house. Day after day, the youngster would bang on the keys, trying to imitate the sounds he had absorbed and turn them into something of his own.

The first song Jerry Lee Lewis played on the piano was the traditional Christmas carol, "Silent Night." Jerry Lee played the song with a definite boogie-woogie beat. His mother exclaimed, "That boy is a natural-born piano player." His father, Elmo, was so pleased that he mortgaged his modest house to buy an old Starck upright piano. Elmo's investment was well-rewarded.

At fourteen, Jerry Lee made his first public appearance, sitting in with a country band in the parking lot of the local Ford automobile dealership. The crowd went wild when he played and sang his version of a recent rhythm and blues song, "Drinkin' Wine Spo-Dee-O-Dee." The owner of the Ford dealership began passing the hat around. By the time Jerry Lee had finished his number, he had earned close to thirteen dollars.

Now that he was a professional musician, Jerry Lee saw no reason to keep attending school. He had never been much of a student anyway, cutting classes more often than not. Now that he had started gaining a reputation as a "hot piano playin' man," Jerry Lee decided to drop out of school completely. In the months that followed, Jerry Lee's father would load the old upright piano on his pickup truck and stop at a corner. Jerry Lee would start to play, and before long a crowd would gather. Elmo passed the hat through the crowd. Then the father-and-son team would move on to another corner. When the day's work was done, they divided up the money.

By this time, Jerry Lee had greatly refined his taste in music. He admired Al Jolson, Jimmy Rodgers, and Hank Williams. Before long, he would brag that outside of these three giants, there was no singer who could top him, or even come close. Jerry Lee was especially moved by black music. There was an interesting contradiction here. On the one hand, Jerry Lee recognized in rhythm and blues the same kind of excitement and frenzy that he had grown up with in the Assembly of God church. On the other hand, he had been warned by his mother that the clubs or juke joints where this music was played were dens of sin. Although this worried the youngster, it did not keep him away.

Jerry Lee got his first real exposure to rhythm and blues at a black nightclub in Ferriday called Haney's Big House. This club featured some of the best bluesmen in the South. Muddy Waters, Ray Charles,

Bobby Bland, B. B. King, and others who were destined to become dominant figures in rhythm and blues in the decades to come played at Haney's regularly. It was the late forties, and the South was still quite segregated. White folks were no more welcome at a black club than black people were at a white nightclub. Yet, Jerry Lee, along with his cousins Mickey Gilley and Jimmy Lee Swaggart, snuck into Haney's with amazing regularity.

Jerry Lee told Nick Tosches, author of *Hellfire*:

> *We'd go down there and sell newspapers and shine shoes . . . and we'd keep on doin' it until nobody was lookin', and then we'd work our way through the door. . . . We'd sneak in there and old Haney, he'd catch us . . . and he'd throw us out. But I sure heard a lot of good piano playin' down there. Man, these old black cats come through in them old buses, feet stickin' out the windows, eatin' sardines. But I tell you, they could really play some music—that's a guaranteed fact.*

It is interesting to note that although Jerry Lee is considered the virtuoso of the family, his two cousins developed piano styles that are almost identical to his own. Today Jimmy Lee Swaggart is a well-known television evangelist, while Mickey Gilley is a popular country singer and nightclub owner. These three cousins — born less than a year apart in the same parish—have pursued their separate paths. But if you happen to catch one of Jimmy Swaggart's gospel piano solos, you'd swear it was Jerry Lee playing. Mickey Gilley's records also have that same kind of piano sound, born in the Assembly of God church and raised during those wild nights at Haney's Big House.

These three famous cousins covered miles and miles of musical territory. But it is the spiritual distance between Jimmy Swaggart's religious calling and Jerry Lee's barroom brawling that offers the most fascinating contrast. Both boys were deeply moved by the great bluesmen they heard at Haney's, but both were also highly religious. Something deep inside kept reminding them that this was the music of Satan.

One spring night in 1950, Elmo Lewis drove Jerry Lee and Jimmy Swaggart to a nearby town to participate in a local talent show. Out of about thirty contestants, Jerry Lee won first prize and Jimmy placed among the top entries. But the future evangelist was distressed by playing what he considered sinful music to a cheering crowd. "For the first time in my life," he was to say later, "I sensed what it felt like to be anointed by the Devil."

Although Jerry Lee had already played in nightclubs, tasted whiskey, and run around with women, he felt a sense of fear and remorse not unlike his cousin's. In what turned out to be the first of several unsuccessful attempts to devote his life to God, Jerry

Lee enrolled at the Southwestern Bible Institute in Waxahachie, Texas.

On the surface, Jerry Lee had many of the qualities needed to become a first-rate preacher. Aside from his extraordinary musical gifts, he was also a fine orator. For brief periods, Jerry Lee actually felt that a religious life might be his calling. But as author Robert Palmer points out in his book, *Jerry Lee Lewis Rocks*, "Those feelings never seemed to last very long, especially not after the sun went down."

It didn't take long for Jerry Lee to start backsliding. Those religious feelings that drove him to Bible College were soon replaced by a longing for the pleasures of the night. Before long, Jerry Lee started sneaking off the campus looking for some action. He soon discovered that there wasn't very much of that kind of thing taking place in Waxahachie. But a half hour away was Dallas, a big city full of all the sins that had caused Jerry Lee to leave home in the first place. In Dallas, he went to movies and amusement parks and snuck into nightclubs. Somehow he sensed that after only three months, his Bible College days were numbered. He described the circumstances of his leaving to Robert Palmer in *Jerry Lee Lewis Rocks*:

*One night, I was playin' "My God Is Real" for a school assembly in the chapel and I played it boogie-woogie style. I had 'em rockin'. I thought that was the way you should do it, but they said, "We can't have this around here. You don't boogie-woogie when you say your prayers at night. You're expelled for two weeks." I said, "I'll take the whole year."*

By the time Jerry Lee returned to Ferriday, he was not overly distressed by his failure to lead a religious life. He soon got a job playing the piano and drums with a blind band leader named Paul Whitehead at a club called the Wagon Wheel. He also met a pretty, dark-haired seventeen-year-old preacher's daughter named Dorothy Barton. Shortly after Jerry Lee turned sixteen, the two were married.

During the first months of his marriage to Dorothy, Jerry Lee once again felt his religious calling. He decided to become a minister, and he began composing sermons. The preacher at the Assembly of God church encouraged him to preach, and for a few Sundays, Jerry Lee took him up on his offer.

In the book *Hellfire*, Nick Tosches describes Jerry Lee's sermons this way:

*Jerry Lee took the pulpit in the little white three-eaved Church of God. He raised his voice and preached about the rich man in hell — how that rich man cried out to Abraham for a drop of water to cool his dry tongue, and how Abraham gave him none, for no man can serve God and Mammon both. Jerry Lee told it to them, and he told it right. People congratulated him, told him he had the makings of a great preacher, that he* was *a great preacher.*

Before long, Jerry Lee started to backslide again. He stopped preaching and started going out at night. Sometime in the spring of 1953, Dorothy decided that she could take no more. She left Jerry Lee and returned to her family. Undaunted, Jerry Lee threw himself into his music, playing and singing at a variety of less than elegant social clubs. Later that summer, he began to work better-paying jobs in the Nachez, Mississippi, area. It was there that he met his second wife, seventeen-year-old Jane Mitcham, who soon became pregnant.

Jane decided that the life of a club musician wasn't a fit one for the future father of her child. She somehow convinced Jerry Lee to take a job as a traveling sewing-maching salesman. Nick Tosches described Jerry Lee's short-lived sales career in *Hellfire*:

> He and another boy roamed through south Louisiana in a 1947 Pontiac that Jerry Lee had acquired. Cruising along, Jerry Lee had one of his fine ideas. He shared this idea with his fellow employee (who) agreed that it was a fine idea; so they executed it.
>
> They went about their business, lugging their sales model sewing machine from door to door. . . . One day, Jerry Lee and his fellow employee stopped off for a Coke and a game of pool at one of those old country stores set way off from any town. In the cracked glass case below the cash register, Jerry Lee noticed a . . . .45 revolver. . . . Sometime after midnight, Jerry Lee and

*his fellow employee returned to the darkened store, hammered open the door, and took the big blue steel .45 out of its case. They got back into the 1947 Pontiac and drove off. They were laughing, playing with the gun, and they didn't see the black-and-white (police) car coming up behing them until it was too late.*

After spending the night in jail, Jerry Lee and his companion stood in front of the local judge. Because of their youth, the judge suspended their sentences and turned them loose.

"It was the last day-job that Jerry Lee ever had," notes Nick Tosches. "He came back to Ferriday and he played piano at the Dixie Club the very same night."

For the next year or so, Jerry Lee continued to work local clubs and improve his reputation. By 1955, he decided that he wanted to try to break into the country music scene. He probably recognized that his style was a bit rough for the Grand Ole Opry, but country still seemed the most likely road for a white boy from the South. His first son, Jerry Lee Lewis, Jr., had been born, and Jerry Lee, Sr., was determined to make some real money with his music.

His first country music sojourn was to Shreveport, Louisiana, to audition for the radio show and package tour, Louisiana Hayride. This was the show that had given Hank Williams his start. Just a few weeks before Jerry Lee showed up, another blues-singing white boy named Elvis Presley had made his successful debut on the Hayride. Unlike Elvis, however, Jerry Lee did not find acceptance and success with the Louisiana Hayride, although he did cut his first demonstration record (demo) there. The demo was cut under the supervision of country singer and Hayride regular Slim Whitman. The songs Jerry Lee chose to record were both current hits—a Hank Snow song called "I Don't Hurt Anymore," and a pop record called "I Need You Now." Although Jerry Lee's performances displayed a strong and distinctive vocal style, Whitman presented him with the demo and curtly said, "Don't call me, I'll call you."

Shortly after this unhappy incident, Jerry Lee gave a well-received performance at the Louisiana State Fair and decided it was time to try his luck at the capital of country music — Nashville. But as anyone who understood the tastes of that great music center in those days could have told him, Jerry Lee just did not fit the picture of what a Nashville country singer was supposed to be. At that time, for example, the Grand Ole Opry did not even allow bands to use drums onstage. A few short months before Jerry Lee showed up, Elvis had made his first guest appearance at the Opry and was told in no uncertain terms that he was not to return.

In *Jerry Lee Lewis Rocks,* Robert Palmer explains why country-rockers like Elvis, Carl Perkins, and Jerry Lee were treated so shabbily by the country music establishment during the mid-fifties. It wasn't that listeners in the South particularly found this music to be so different from what they were used to. Certainly, these young men were shaking their bodies and playing music that was more hopped up than most of what was then being played on country stations. However, there was a rebellion taking place. And, as Palmer points out, a healthy portion of it "(was) directed at the country music industry and the established stars of the preceding generation — the Roy Acuffs and Hank Snows":

> *Jerry Lee Lewis and Elvis Presley and the other budding rockers of their generation got the cold shoulder in Nashville until Presley returned there a star. Most of the older country singers had firsthand knowledge of the honky-tonk life, but they were appalled, or at best bemused, by these youngsters who . . . wiggled their hips at their audiences, fell down on all fours and pounded the stage with their fists or jumped on top of pianos. . . .*
>
> *(Jerry Lee) could have probably pounded on Nashville office doors and auditioned for radio shows and talent agencies there forever without getting anywhere; Nashville had found a proven formula for success, an increasingly slick, uptown, country-and-western sound, and the ideas was to find artists who could fit smoothly into the formula, not artists who would trash it.*

It is not at all surprising that Jerry Lee eventually found success in Memphis with Sam Phillips's Sun Records. Although Phillips's small recording studio was the only one in the entire city of Memphis, it was the place where Elvis had recorded his early ground-breaking music. When Phillips sold Elvis's contract to RCA records for $35,000 in 1955, he began looking for another young artist with similar talent and mass appeal. It wasn't only the sound that Phillips sought— a cross between country twang and blues-based rhythms — but also the kind of presence and magnetism that drove audiences wild. Other Sun artists like Carl Perkins and Johnny Cash had hit records, but neither of these fine singers could move an audience the way Elvis could.

Every day when Sam Phillips walked into his studio, there were hundreds of letters and demo tapes from young men who were certain that *they* were the next Elvis Presley. When Jerry Lee returned empty-handed from Nashville, he knew that the Sun recording studio in Memphis had to be his next stop. Elmo Lewis sold thirty-three dozen eggs to finance the trip. He and Jerry Lee drove to Memphis, straight to 706 Union Avenue. At the time, Sam Phillips was out of town on business. Jerry Lee and Elmo were received—with something less than open arms—by Jack Clement, a young producer Phillips had hired to assist him.

Clement was experienced in discouraging young hopefuls who parked themselves on Sun's doorstep. But Jerry Lee wasn't about to be turned away. "I told them I was going to get an audition," he recalls, "if I had to sit on the doorstep for three weeks." One of the things that made Jerry Lee seem a bit different to Clement was the fact that he played piano, not guitar. Clement consented to put a few of Jerry Lee's songs on tape, and he was sufficiently impressed to play them for Sam Phillips. The owner of Sun Records recalls his first reaction in *Jerry Lee Lewis Rocks*:

> *Jack Clement . . . put this tape on, "Crazy Arms," and I said, "Where . . . did this man come from?" He played that piano with abandon. A lot of people do that, but I could hear, between the stuff he played and didn't play, that spiritual thing. Jerry is very spiritual. I said, "Jack, did you get his . . . phone number?" He said, "Yeah, I know where he is." I said, "Well, you get him in here as fast as you can." It was as if someone had read my mind about having a soloist on piano and getting off this guitar scene.*

"Crazy Arms" got some local attention, but Sam Phillips understood that the kind of song Jerry Lee needed was not a country ballad, but one that crossed all musical boundaries. In the meantime, Phillips employed Jerry Lee's considerable piano playing talents on recordings and performances of other Sun artists. All the while, Jerry Lee kept sharpening his own talents, confident that he would soon be rewarded with a hit record.

In April 1957, Jerry Lee recorded his second Sun single. Originally, the A side of the record was a Jack Clement song called "It'll Be Me." The flip side was a tune Jerry Lee had been playing in clubs since 1955, "Whole Lotta Shakin' Goin' On." The record was first released in the South, and it was immediately apparent that teenage record buyers preferred "Whole Lotta Shakin'. . . ." Sam Phillips recognized that here was a record that had the potential of going straight to the top. But there were some problems. Many radio stations received complaints that the song was too suggestive, and they banned it.

Jerry Lee was now being managed by Judd Phillips, Sam's brother. Judd realized that "Whole Lotta Shakin'. . ." was Sun's hottest property. Somehow, he had to let the world see and hear Jerry Lee perform this tune. Judd Phillips took Jerry Lee up to New York and got him on the nationally syndicated Steve Allen show. Nick Tosches describes that breakthrough performance in *Hellfire*:

> . . . *With less than five minutes left to the show, Jerry Lee was given his signal. He sat at the big piano and he looked sideways at the camera. . . . Then he began to play the piano and howl about the shaking that was going on. He rose, still pounding, and he kicked the piano stool back. It shot across the stage. . . .*

*Steve Allen laughed and threw the stool back, then threw other furniture, and Jerry Lee played some high notes with the heel of his shoe. Then he stopped and looked at the camera sideways again. Neither he nor Steve Allen had ever heard louder applause.*

Jerry Lee's career began to explode at this point. By the end of the summer, "Whole Lotta Shakin'. . ." reached the top of the country, pop, and rhythm and blues charts. Jerry Lee returned to his home in Ferriday with a smile on his face and money in his pocket. He bought his parents a new house in a better part of town. He put together a little band consisting of Russell Smith on drums and J. W. Brown on bass guitar, and they played concerts all over America. Jerry Lee was now earning upwards of a thousand dollars a night, plus he had thousands more in record royalties coming in each week. By the time his next hit single, "Great Balls of Fire," hit the stores in the fall, some people were saying that Jerry Lee had unseated Elvis as the king of rock and roll.

The time was right for Jerry Lee to become the hottest performer in America. Elvis was about to go into the Army, and many people felt that his records had already begun to lose their bite. Jerry Lee, on the other hand, was sizzling. "Great Balls of Fire" had done almost as well as "Whole Lotta Shakin'. . . ." His next two singles—"Breathless"and "High School

Confidential" — were released about twelve weeks apart. There were a lot more recordings "in the can" awaiting the right time for release.

Sam Phillips was pleased. Not only had he found a rock and roller who thrilled the teenagers, he truly believed that Jerry Lee was one of the best country singers he had ever heard. And Phillips had the recordings sitting in his vault to prove it. Here was a talent, Phillips felt, who could be at the forefront of American music for generations to come. Then, disaster struck.

As great a talent as Jerry Lee Lewis is, his personal life has always managed to overshadow his music. During the height of his success, he set a piano on fire because he was angry that the promoters chose Chuck Berry to follow him on stage. Jerry Lee had nothing personal against Berry. He just firmly believed that there wasn't an entertainer on earth good enough to follow him on stage. Jerry Lee has also been known to physically assault hecklers who jeer him from the audience. His bouts with alcohol and pills are so legendary that his cousin Jimmy Lee Swaggart has often said, "Every time the phone rings, I'm afraid to answer it because I think it will be someone calling to say that Jerry Lee is dead." Jerry Lee has lost more money in lawsuits than most people could earn in twenty lifetimes. But the scandal Jerry Lee is most famous for is his marriage to thirteen-year-old Myra Brown in 1958.

It is important to keep in mind that during the fifties, many people considered rock and roll to be evil, immoral music. Although Myra was extremely young, it was not so unusual for a girl in that part of the South to marry at that age. The fact that she was Jerry Lee's cousin and the daughter of his bass player did little to help the situation. Jerry Lee and his troupe had begun an English tour in late May 1958. When the British press learned of Jerry Lee's marriage, they did a hatchet job on his career that has rarely been equaled since. After all the bad publicity forced the cancellation of the remainder of his tour, Jerry Lee returned to his homeland, where the American newspapers had their turn. In an attempt to stem the tide, Jerry Lee ran an "open letter" in all the music trade publications. It read in part:

> I sincerely want to be worthy of the decent admiration of all the people, young and old, that admired what talent (if any) I had. ... I can cry all I want to but I can't control the press or the sensationalism that these people will go to to get a story started to sell papers. If you don't believe me then you can ask any of the other people who have been victims of the same.

For the next several years, Jerry Lee watched his career sink like a stone. Radio stations refused to play his records; television shows like Dick Clark's "American Bandstand" banned him; and—perhaps worst of all—his record company did not stand behind him. It may be true, as Jerry Lee has often claimed, that if Sun Records hadn't panicked, the entire incident would have blown over in a few months. As Colin Escott noted in a booklet that accompanied the release of a twelve-album set called *Jerry Lee Lewis: The Sun Years:*

> *Realistically, the fiasco in England had done no more than expedite the inevitable. Jerry was almost the last of a dying breed. Hard rockers were becoming noticeably absent from the charts and the radio. Middle America was fighting back with a vengeance and Jerry Lee with his blues-drenched music, his . . . unseemly long hair and wild and wooly ways stood . . . (little) chance of surviving the new market conditions. It is true that Elvis survived but he had a stint in the Army to improve his image, more versatility as a performer, a sharper manager, and the concern of RCA to protect their investment.*

The next eight years were tough ones for Jerry Lee. He released some more records on Sun, but nothing much happened. In 1963, he signed a five-year deal with Smash Records, but there were no smashes. Jerry Lee supported himself primarily by working clubs that featured entertainers on their way up or on their way down, and as one magazine writer curtly put it: "Jerry Lee Lewis had already been up." Then, in 1967, Jerry Lee and his producer Jerry Kennedy promised the top country music disc jockeys that if they would play Jerry Lee's records, he would confine his recording career to country only. For the next few years, rebellious Jerry Lee Lewis was one of Nashville's biggest stars.

His first country hit, "Another Place, Another Time," was a classic country lament that quickly shot up to number one on the country hit parade. Unlike many of the slow songs that were coming out of Nashville at that time, Jerry Lee's record was gutty and heartfelt, not sentimental and syrupy. This was

Jerry Lee on guitar—talent, versatility, and flamboyance.

followed by a series of country hits including: "What's Made Milwaukee Famous (Has Made a Loser Out of Me)," "She Still Comes Around (To Love What's Left of Me)," "She Even Woke Me Up to Say Goodbye," and "Would You Take Another Chance On Me."

This change in musical direction may have been a brilliant piece of career strategy, but it was sincere just the same. This was, after all, the music Jerry Lee had grown up with. As he told *Rolling Stone*'s Peter Guralnick in 1970: "I've always sung country music . . . all my life. The only thing is I'm a little more serious about it now."

True to his word, Jerry Lee has kept his recordings strictly in a country vein, although he still performs rock and roll live. His importance to both musical styles is undeniable. But at this point, his influence is more apparent in country.

Jerry Lee — as much as any contemporary performer — creates music in the tradition of the great country giants. When he sings a Jimmy Rodgers song like "Waitin' For a Train," he yodels with the best of them. And when he sings a Hank Williams tune like "You Win Again," there can be no doubt about his sincerity or his real-life experiences with love gone sour (Jerry Lee has been married five times). Like all great country singers, Jerry Lee's music is an expression of his real emotions.

During the past few years, Jerry Lee has alternated between hit country records, rock and roll concerts, lawsuits, and hospital stays resulting from self-abuse. Perhaps it's just a coincidence, but Jerry Lee began another resurgence in 1977, right after Elvis died. One song he cut around that time, "Middle-Age Crazy," was his biggest hit in years and the basis for a movie. Jerry Lee's records still grace the charts, though perhaps not as often as his name appears in gossip columns. Nevertheless, his place as a country music superstar is secure.

One matter that Jerry Lee has been complaining about since the fifties is the lack of recognition he receives compared to other singers. The way he tells it, he has never even been approached, much less surpassed, by anyone living. This kind of talk makes him sound vain and ridiculous at times, although no one can ever accuse him of being less than honest about his feelings.

Jerry Lee's vital contributions to at least two great American musical traditions—country and rock and roll—can never be minimized. He was one of the great young talents who combined country music and blues to create rock and roll in the fifties. More than a decade later, he injected a much needed dose of vitality into a country music scene that was getting a bit stale. As much as anyone, he helped people understand how close different forms of American music really are.

What can we expect from Jerry Lee Lewis in the future? One never knows. He is now with MCA, his fourth record label. His recent records and performances have been a bit more subdued. Whether this is due to maturity or weariness is hard to determine. But this man whose life has encompassed the greatest extremes of religion and sin, and who has covered a musical territory that is almost as wide, probably still has a few surprises left.

"I'll keep on bein' the greatest show on earth till they put me six feet under," the man they call "The Killer" told *Esquire*. "And even then, I might still find a way to keep hangin' it in."

# Jerry Lee Lewis Collector's Guide

| YEAR | ALBUM | LABEL |
|------|-------|-------|
| 1964 | The Golden Hits of Jerry Lee Lewis | Smash/Mercury |
| 1964 | The Greatest Live Show on Earth | Smash/Mercury |
| 1965 | The Return of Rock | Smash/Mercury |
| 1966 | Memphis Beat | Smash/Mercury |
| 1968 | Another Place, Another Time | Smash/Mercury |
| 1969 | She Still Comes Around (To Love What's Left of Me) | Smash/Mercury |
| 1969 | The Country Music Hall of Fame Volume I | Smash/Mercury |
| 1969 | The Country Music Hall of Fame Volume II | Smash/Mercury |
| 1969 | Together (with Linda Gail) | Smash/Mercury |
| 1969 | Original Golden Hits Volume I | Sun |
| 1969 | Original Golden Hits Volume II | Sun |
| 1970 | She Even Woke Me Up To Say Goodbye | Smash/Mercury |
| 1970 | Live at the International Las Vegas | Mercury |
| 1970 | Taste of Country | Sun |
| 1970 | Rockin' Rhythm and Blues | Sun |
| 1970 | Sunday Down South (with Johnny Cash) | Sun |
| 1970 | Old Tyme Country Music | Sun |
| 1971 | There Must Be More To Love Than This | Mercury |
| 1971 | Loving Memories | Mercury |
| 1971 | Monsters | Sun |

| YEAR | ALBUM | LABEL |
|------|-------|-------|
| 1971 | Sings Hank Williams (with Johnny Cash) | Sun |
| 1971 | Touching Home | Mercury |
| 1971 | Would You Take Another Chance On Me | Mercury |
| 1972 | The Killer Rocks On | Mercury |
| 1972 | Original Golden Hits Volume III | Sun |
| 1973 | This Old Piano | Mercury |
| 1973 | Session | Mercury |
| 1973 | Session in London | Mercury/Capital |
| 1973 | Sometimes a Memory Ain't Enough | Mercury |
| 1974 | Southern Roots | Mercury |
| 1974 | The Junkie and the Juicehead Minus Me | Columbia |
| 1976 | Odd Man In | Mercury |
| 1976 | Country Class | Mercury |
| 1977 | Country Memories | Mercury |
| 1978 | The Best of Jerry Lee Lewis Volume II | Sun |
| 1978 | Jerry Lee Lewis Keeps Rockin' | Sun |
| 1979 | Duets With Friends (with Charles Rich and Carl Perkins) | Sun |
| 1979 | Jerry Lee Lewis | Elektra |
| 1980 | When Two Worlds Collide | Elektra |
| 1980 | Killer Country | Elektra |
| 1981 | Golden Hits | Elektra |
| 1982 | The Survivors (with Johnny Cash and Carl Perkins) | Columbia |
| 1982 | The Best of Jerry Lee Lewis | Elektra |
| 1983 | My Fingers Do the Talkin' | MCA |
| 1983 | Jerry Lee Lewis The Killer Nov. 1956–Aug. 1963 (12 record set) | Charly Records |

| YEAR | SINGLE | LABEL | C&W | POP |
|------|--------|-------|-----|-----|
| 1956 | Crazy Arms/End of the Road | Sun | | |
| 1957 | Whole Lotta Shakin' Going On | Sun | * | x* |
| 1957 | Great Balls of Fire | Sun | * | x* |
| 1958 | Breathless | Sun | * | x* |
| 1958 | You Win Again | Sun | | x |
| 1958 | High School Confidential | Sun | * | x |
| 1958 | Break Up | Sun | | x |
| 1958 | I'll Make It All Up To You | Sun | | x |
| 1959 | I'll Sail My Ship Alone | Sun | | x |
| 1961 | What I Say | Sun | | x |
| 1961 | Cold, Cold Heart | Sun | | |
| 1962 | Sweet Little Sixteen | Sun | | |
| 1964 | I'm On Fire | Smash/Mercury | | x |
| 1964 | High Heel Sneakers | Smash/Mercury | | x |
| 1964 | Pen and Paper | Smash/Mercury | | |
| 1968 | Another Place, Another Time | Smash/Mercury | * | x |
| 1968 | What's Made Milwaukee Famous (Has Made a Loser Out Of Me) | Smash/Mercury | * | x |
| 1968 | She Still Comes Around | Smash/Mercury | * | |
| 1968 | To Make Love Sweeter For You | Smash/Mercury | * | |
| 1969 | Invitation To Your Party | Sun | * | |
| 1969 | One Minute Past Eternity | Sun | * | |
| 1969 | Don't Let Me Cross Over (with Linda Gail) | Smash/Mercury | * | |
| 1969 | One Has My Name | Smash/Mercury | * | |
| 1969 | She Even Woke Me Up To Say Goodbye | Smash/Mercury | * | |
| 1970 | I Can't Seem To Say Goodbye | Sun | | |

* Smash Hit
X Crossover to Pop

| YEAR | SINGLE | LABEL | C&W | POP |
|------|--------|-------|-----|-----|
| 1970 | Waiting for a Train | Sun | | |
| 1970 | Roll Over Beethoven (with Linda Gail) | Smash/Mercury | | |
| 1970 | Once More with Feeling | Smash/Mercury | * | |
| 1970 | There Must Be More To Love Than This | Mercury | * | |
| 1971 | Love On Broadway | Sun | | |
| 1971 | In Loving Memories | Mercury | * | |
| 1971 | Touching Home | Mercury | * | |
| 1971 | When He Walks On You (Like You Walked On Me) | Mercury | | |
| 1971 | Me and Bobby McGee | Mercury | | x |
| 1971 | Would You Take Another Chance On Me | Mercury | * | |
| 1972 | Chantilly Lace/Think About It Darlin' | Mercury | * | x |
| 1972 | Lonely Weekends | Mercury | | |
| 1972 | Turn On Your Lovelight | Mercury | | x |
| 1972 | Who's Gonna Play This Old Piano | Mercury | | |
| 1973 | No More Hanging On | Mercury | | |
| 1973 | No Headstone On My Grave | Mercury | | |
| 1973 | Sometimes a Memory Ain't Enough | Mercury | * | |
| 1974 | I'm Left, You're Right, She's Gone | Mercury | | |
| 1974 | Tell Tale Signs | Mercury | | |
| 1974 | He Can't Fill My Shoes | Mercury | * | |
| 1975 | I Can Still Hear the Music in the Restroom | Mercury | | |
| 1975 | Boogie-Woogie Country Man | Mercury | | |
| 1975 | A Dam Good Country Song | Mercury | | |
| 1976 | Don't Boogie-Woogie | Mercury | | |
| 1976 | Let's Put It Back Together Again | Mercury | * | |
| 1976 | The Closest Thing To You | Mercury | | |

| YEAR | SINGLE | LABEL | C&W | POP |
|------|--------|-------|-----|-----|
| 1977 | Middle-Age Crazy | Mercury | | * |
| 1978 | Come On It | Mercury | | * |
| 1978 | I'll Find It Where I Can | Mercury | | * |
| 1979 | Rockin' My Life Away/I Wish I Was Eighteen Again | Elektra | | |
| 1979 | Cold, Cold Heart | Sun | | |
| 1979 | Who Will The Next Fool Be | Elektra | | |
| 1980 | When Two Worlds Collide | Elektra | | |
| 1980 | Honky-Tonk Stuff | Elektra | | |
| 1980 | Over the Rainbow | Elektra | | * |
| 1980 | 39 and Holding | Elektra | | * |
| 1982 | I'm So Lonesome I Could Cry | Mercury | | |
| 1982 | I'll Do It All Again | Elektra | | |
| 1982 | My Fingers Do the Talkin' | MCA | | * |
| 1983 | Why You Been Gone So Long | MCA | | |

* Smash Hit
X Crossover to Pop

Tammy Wynette—a bona fide country music queen.

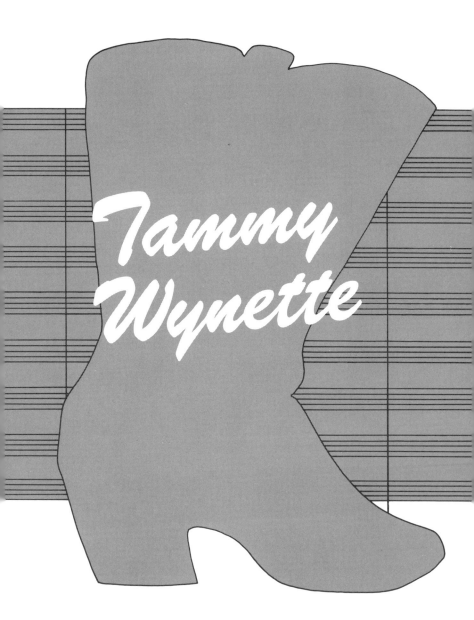

Tammy Wynette

*If I hadn't had hurdles along the way, I wouldn't fully appreciate my success.*

          *Tammy Wynette*, Stand By Your Man

What are the qualities that turn a good country singer into a bona fide superstar? Is it extraordinary musical talent, good looks, timing, luck, or a combination of all these factors? The exact formula is different in every case. Some superstars have more of one and less of another. But Tammy Wynette apparently has it all. She was born with a tremendous amount of talent. Many critics rate her as the top female singer in country music. She has the looks of a movie star. Considering that she arrived in Nashville with no connections at a time when female country singers were not exactly a hot item, you'd have to say her timing turned out to be pretty good. Finally, despite their highly publicized marital problems, her relationship with country music legend George Jones gave her the confidence and credibility to go straight to the top.

There's more to the story, though—a lot more. Tammy Wynette strikes a chord in her audiences, particularly the women, that accounts for the legions of fanatical fans who constitute the backbone of her phenomenally successful career. Tammy has always been mindful of how much her fans mean to her career. As she says in her autobiography, *Stand By Your Man:*

> *In the record business, you're only as good as your last hit or as important as your next one. . . . If you stop recording hits, your label will eventually drop you, but the country music fans don't. If you've recorded just one song that they remember and love, you can go on getting bookings the rest of your life.*

As any country music fan knows, Tammy Wynette has given her fans much more than one hit song to love. Since she recorded her first single in 1966, "Apartment Number Nine," her songs have reached the number-one spot in the country charts thirty-five times. "Stand By Your Man," a song she co-wrote with her producer Billy Sherrill, is one of the biggest-selling records in the history of country music. Her numerous honors include two Grammies, three Country Music Association awards as the Top Female Vocalist of the Year, and over a dozen citations for her songwriting. Above and beyond her outstanding musical talent, Tammy is so well loved by her fans because they recognize something about themselves in her music and her personal life.

Tammy was born Virginia Wynette Pugh on May 5, 1942. When she was eight months old, her father died of a brain tumor, and she was raised by her grandparents. Tammy's father had been a musician of sorts. Before his death, he requested that if his baby daughter showed any inclination toward music, she be encouraged to pursue it.

Although her family wasn't extremely poor, Tammy began picking cotton at age seven. All the while, she thought about her father's wish that she someday make music her life. This became her escape from the long, back-breaking hours in the cotton fields.

One of Tammy's fantasies as she worked in the hot sun was that she would someday appear in front of thousands of people singing a duet with her idol, George Jones. Although such thoughts seemed far-fetched at the time, Tammy did exhibit a great deal of musical talent as a youngster. She began playing piano and singing long before she began taking formal music lessons. By the time she was eight, Tammy was playing piano at the local Baptist church. She recalls that the preacher asked someone in the congregation to replace the previous piano player who had recently passed away. Tammy volunteered without hesitation. "I knew all the old hymns by heart," she remembers. "and I wanted to be up there making music."

Tammy never forgot the musical experiences she had in church. The church was a center of social life for the entire community, and Tammy became well known to the members of the congregation for her musical talents. It was in church where she learned how to harmonize and how to perform in front of an audience: "I get much the same feeling today when I perform on stage that I did then singing in front of the congregation," she says in her autobiography. "It's a kind of thrill that never gets stale."

When she was in her teens, Tammy started her own vocal trio and sang on a local radio show. But she had another dream that at times was even stronger than her fantasy of becoming a professional singer. She wanted to get married and have babies. When two of her friends got married during her senior year in high school, Tammy followed suit. "I mistook infatuation for love," she freely admits now. "I thought marriage would get me off the farm."

Tammy did succeed in leaving her grandfather's farm. But she found that life with her first husband, Euple Byrd, was even more depressing than picking cotton. She had given birth to two daughters within three years. But Euple was out of work more often than not, and there was little money coming in. Eventually, the near destitute family was forced to move into an abandoned log cabin. There was no stove or running water, but at least it was rent-free. "Not even the poorest sharecropper would have paid to live there," Tammy recalls.

Eventually, Euple got a steady job, and the family moved into a real house with indoor plumbing.

Tammy had almost stopped thinking about her music career. Instead, she decided to go to beauty school so that she could help improve her family's meager standard of living. No sooner had she scraped the money together to begin classes when Euple quit his job and moved the family to Memphis.

One day Tammy was walking on Front Street in Memphis with her two children when she heard the sound of country music coming out of a bar. Although she had never been inside a bar in her life, she couldn't resist the music. The owners of the bar invited her in and offered her a job as a barmaid. Eventually, the owners asked Tammy to sing the customers' requests for tips. The man who owned the bar was a good blues piano player. One night he called Tammy over and said, "You've got a good voice, but you're strictly country. You belong in Nashville."

Tammy claims that this was the first time she had actually thought about going to Nashville. At this point in her life, she was much more concerned with getting her beautician's license so that she could earn some steady money. Even today, after all her triumphs, she still keeps that license renewed. "I guess I still think getting paid to sing is too good to be true," she explains in her autobiography. "And if it ends tomorrow I can always go back to doing hair."

Soon after getting her beautician's license, Tammy moved to Birmingham, Alabama, where she gave birth to her third daughter. She had moved to divorce Euple, and she was working ten hours a day in a beauty shop, but her music career had finally begun to show some signs of life.

There was a local television show in Birmingham called "Country Boy Eddie." It was aired on weekdays from 6 to 7 A.M. Tammy used to watch the show when she dressed for work, and she noticed that they didn't feature a female singer. As it happened, an uncle of hers was an engineer at the station. He arranged for an audition, and Tammy got the job. Although she was thrilled with the opportunity, the pay was only thirty-five dollars a week, not nearly enough to quit the beauty shop. This meant that she had to get up at four in the morning in order to take care of the children and dress for the show. The hours were tough, but at least she was making progress with her music.

Tammy understood that if she was really going to make her mark as a singer, she would have to go to Nashville. She began taking time off from work and driving the 200 miles from Birmingham to make the rounds of record companies in Nashville. Although she had great confidence in her talent, she did not know how to present herself to a record company.

When a singer wants to get heard, he or she usually makes a demonstration tape (demo) and presents it to potentially interested record companies and producers. Tammy figured that she would just walk in off the street and get some guidance from a music business professional. Today it is virtually impossible to get in to see someone in the music business without an appointment. But things were a little looser in 1965, and Tammy actually did get to audition for a few small companies. Nothing came of those early auditions, however, and Tammy soon found herself working at the beauty shop again.

During that period in her life, Tammy lucked into a situation that she hoped would be her golden opportunity. Country music star Porter Wagoner was performing in Birmingham and was in need of a female singer. Wagoner had one of the most popular road shows in country music. One of his trademarks was a featured woman singer. His previous vocalist of seven years, Norma Jean, had just retired from touring, and he had not yet hooked up with Dolly Parton, who was to become an important part of his act for years to come. When a local radio station recommended Tammy for the opening, she was certain this was the break for which she had been waiting.

Tammy claims that Wagoner was sitting in his dressing room, and she is not altogether sure that he even heard her sing. After she performed, Wagoner thanked her and shook her hand, but said nothing about working together. Tammy was feeling kind of depressed when a member of the tour told her that Wagoner would pay her fifty dollars a night to sing with him for the next ten days. Although Wagoner would not allow her to travel on the bus with the rest of the band, Tammy felt confident that after the ten days had passed, she would be offered a permanent job.

Unfortunately, things did not work out the way Tammy wanted them to. Wagoner and the rest of his band were very polite to her, but no job offer was forthcoming. To make matters worse, Wagoner never once indicated that he felt Tammy had the goods to make it as a country singer. He simply said, "thank you and goodbye." The very next day, Tammy was back at her job at the beauty parlor.

"I had always enjoyed doing hair before that," she recalls in her autobiography, "but after being on the road, I hated it so much by comparison that it took every bit of self-discipline I could muster to drag myself out of bed in the morning. I thought I'd scream if I saw one more hair roller or smelled one more bottle of permanent wave solution."

Although she was discouraged, Tammy was more determined than ever to make it as a singer. She had gotten her first taste of the road, and she was totally convinced that this was the life she was destined to lead. Tammy decided to pull out all the stops in order to launch her career. This meant giving up her job, loading her three small children into the car, and moving to Nashville.

Those first few months in "Music City, U.S.A." felt more like Poverty City. "Livin' in a one-room efficiency in Nashville on my own with three kids, an old beat-up car, no work and nobody to call for help had to be the lowest point in my life," Tammy told *Interview* magazine. "I couldn't buy anything. It was hard enough just keepin' food on the table. We had hot biscuits and gravy for breakfast and cornbread and milk at night. That was all we had to eat. That went on for six or eight months."

Tammy may not have known any powerful people in Nashville, but she was not at all shy when it came to presenting herself. She just pounded the pavement, auditioning for anyone who would listen. A few people encouraged Tammy, but no recording contract was offered. Producers and record companies could only take on a very small percentage of the singers who wanted to record. The odds were even worse for women, who were not yet considered proven moneymakers in country music.

"You're good," record producers would tell Tammy. "But we already have a girl singer on our label." That was the response Tammy received when she went to audition for a producer named Kelso Hurston, who was working with a female singer named Billie Jo Spears. "But there is someone else in Nashville you should go see," Hurston told Tammy.

"His name is Billy Sherrill. . . . He just might be ready to sign a girl singer."

When Tammy walked into Billy Sherrill's office with her three daughters in tow, she had no idea that this would turn out to be the break for which she had been waiting. Sherrill was one of Nashville's hottest, up-and-coming, young record producers and songwriters. Tammy was lucky to have been able to just walk into his office without an appointment. Normally, a name producer would not even devote five minutes to an unknown singer without a demo to present. But Tammy Wynette was not typical. She proceeded to borrow a guitar from Sherrill and sing a couple of recent hits for him.

"He didn't say anything at all for a minute or two," Tammy recalls in her autobiography. "Then he spoke in a very matter-of-fact tone: 'I don't have time to look for material for you, but if you can come up with a good song, I'll record you.'"

The very next day, Tammy began going around to song publishing companies looking for a song to record. She quickly found one that Sherrill liked. It was called "She Didn't Color Daddy." Sherrill had found an even better song, however, entitled "Apartment Number Nine." As soon as Tammy heard it, she knew that it was going to be a hit for her. Sherrill scheduled recording time for the following week. Only one thing bothered him: he didn't think Wynette Pugh was a very good name for a country superstar in the making. He thought about it for a moment, then he said, "With that blonde ponytail you look like a Tammy to me."

"Can I at least keep Wynette?" she asked hopefully.

"Sure," answered Billy Sherrill. "How about Tammy Wynette?"

"Apartment Number Nine" was an instant hit, and Tammy's next eleven singles all made it to number one. Within three short years, she had won her first Grammy and her first two awards as the Country Music Association's Female Vocalist of the Year. She also divorced her second husband, songwriter Don Chapel, around that time. Tammy had fallen deeply in love with one of her girlhood idols, country music legend George Jones.

Although he has never been as popular with national audiences as some other country performers, George Jones has been a major force in country music since the mid-fifties. Country music historians like Bill Malone, author of *Country Music U.S.A.,* feel that Jones's intensely personal vocal style and songwriting put him on a level with greats like Jimmy Rodgers and Hank Williams in the all-time country music hierarchy.

Since Tammy grew up worshiping George Jones, imagine how thrilled she was when she became an opening act for him. Tammy began singing duets with George onstage, and one thing led to another. Eventually, they got married. They became the hottest musical duet *and* the hottest gossip item in country music history. During the six years they were together, Tammy and George recorded a string of hit records. They toured together, lived together, and sang together. Although they were happy for a time, George Jones periodically went on long, highly publicized drinking sprees. When Tammy could no longer take any more, she reluctantly filed for her third divorce. The union between Tammy and George produced one child, Tamela Georgette.

The publicity from her relationship with George Jones sparked a tremendous amount of discussion about Tammy's personal life. Although country performers pride themselves on their sincerity, record companies and press agents use whatever they can from an entertainer's personal life to fuel their public image. When Tammy Wynette sings "Stand By Your Man," the obvious question is how come she keeps divorcing all her husbands? This is not an easy question for a public figure to answer. Tammy says that she really wants to stand by her man. With her fifth marriage to songwriter/producer George Richey, Tammy is certain that she has finally found personal happiness. "No way anyone or anything can come between me and my marriage," she told *People*. "I've never been so happy."

It is important that listeners understand that singers are *not* 100 percent accountable for the songs they sing any more than actors are accountable for the roles they play. In fact, it is probably more accurate to think of a singer as a kind of actor who understands the emotions she sings about. Still, Tammy admits that one of her favorite recordings is "D-I-V-O-R-C-E," while one of her least favorites is "Stand By Your Man." According to Tammy, she only recorded the song because her producer, Billy Sherrill, insisted that it was right. "Billy is always right," she has said many times. "If he came in and told me to record 'Yankee Doodle,' I'd do it."

Billy Sherrill has built a reputation as one of Nashville's premier producers and songwriters. He has been instrumental in molding the careers of Tammy, Tanya Tucker, and Charlie Rich. He has also worked with such luminaries as the late Marty Robbins, Barbara Mandrell, and Kris Kristofferson. But Sherrill's talents are not only musical. He is what is known in the music industry as an image builder.

From the start, Sherrill sensed that Tammy had tremendous appeal for women. Her storybook marriage to George Jones, her four divorces, her involvement with stars like Burt Reynolds, only enhanced the image Sherrill envisioned for her. Just as Loretta Lynn is presented as a woman who is outspoken about women's rights, Tammy is presented as a vulnerable victim of unhappy love. To a great extent, these are just images for the public to hang its hat on, not true pictures of real people.

To have made it as a woman in a tough, competitive arena like country music, you can bet that Tammy Wynette had a lot of personal strength and fierce independence. Her image may not please the women's movement as much as that of some other singers, but her actual behavior is an example to anyone with a dream of success. In her autobiography, Tammy discusses her struggle for recognition:

*In (the sixties) there weren't more than a half-dozen women headlining their own shows in country music. . . . Every time one of us stood up for our rights, she made a point for all of us. We had our own "liberation movement" going, but I don't think any of us was aware of it. All I wanted was the right to work in my chosen field and be treated with the same respect as the men who did the same job. Those few of us who were out there working in the sixties had to work extra hard to prove to the bookers and promoters, as well as the male entertainers, that we could*

**229**

*handle the business and hardships of the road as well as they could. We also had to prove we could bring in audiences. As a result of our success, a female singer starting out in country music today (has it much easier). Things have improved 100 percent and I'm proud I played a part in making that happen.*

No matter how you characterize Tammy Wynette—strong-minded career woman or soap-opera-style victim of love—you cannot deny the powerful spell she casts when she sings. "No country music singer conveys emotion more poignantly," writes Joan Dew in *Singers & Sweethearts—The Women in Country Music*. "Whenever Tammy performs—auditorium or nightclub—the audience is mesmerized . . . Her tearful singing style is the voice of every heartbreak a woman has ever known."

Tammy recognizes her ability to communicate as the key to her tremendous success. "A woman is a woman regardless of what city or country she lives in," Tammy told *Interview* magazine:

> *She still has the same feelings and goes through the same experiences. . . . I feel that I can really relate to the average woman because I myself feel very average. I worked as a waitress. I worked in a bank. I worked in a shoe factory. I worked picking cotton. I worked as a receptionist. There are so many ordinary jobs that I've done that the ordinary woman makes her living doing. And I always associate myself with the average woman.*

Tammy's ability to communicate doesn't stop with her singing. She is widely recognized as an accomplished songwriter. Tammy has written or co-written hits not only for herself but for other artists as well. For example, she wrote, "Those Days I Barely Get By," "The Bottle," and "I Just Stopped By To See If I Was Gone" for ex-husband George Jones. She also wrote, "That's The Way It Could Have Been" for Kenny Rogers and Dottie West. Tammy refers to songwriting as "a form of therapy" and "the best way I know to get something off my chest."

Although Tammy was writing and recording hits before she met George Jones, it has taken time for her to emerge from his enormous shadow. "When we were married, I depended on George to carry the ball onstage," she admits, "because he was more at ease fooling around with an audience. I only felt comfortable when I was singing. . . . Now I feel at home with them and I use my music to share intimacies I would have been afraid to share a few years ago."

These days Tammy is considerably more popular than her former husband and idol. Ironically, her current husband, George Richey, has written songs for and assisted Jones in his career. Tammy and George are still good friends. After the pain of their separation subsided, they continued recording together. In fact, some critics think they made their best music *after* the divorce. "Our marriage didn't work," Tammy explains. "But that's the only thing that didn't work. George and I never lost respect for each other. We always worked well professionally."

Today Tammy is still turning out country hits. Although some of her records don't cross over to the pop charts as often as Dolly Parton's or Crystal Gayle's, Tammy was responsible for making many rock fans aware of country music. "Stand By Your Man" was the only country song in the soundtrack of the enormously popular and influential 1967 film, *Easy Rider*. In a soundtrack that featured rock artists like the Band, the Byrds, and Jimi Hendrix, Tammy opened many new ears to country music.

Tammy spends about half of each month on the road. She is accompanied on every booking by her husband, who has given up much of his own career to supervise hers. Tammy spends as much time as possible with her four daughters. She has homes in Florida and Nashville, where she has business interests in a variety of ventures. Even though she'll never have to pick cotton again, Tammy still claims to get a back-ache every time she passes a cotton field.

"I made up my mind that I'd do anything before I'd go back to that life," she says in her autobiography. "But I never dreamed then that 'anything' would turn out to be the one thing I loved doing most of all—singing."

During her early days knocking on doors in Nashville, Tammy dreamed of someday making her living in music. She could never have envisioned the degree of success she has achieved. But with all the money, adulation, and publicity, she has not lost her perspective. As she told *Interview*:

> *The only way success has changed us at all is that we have a bigger house to live in and more food. (On the other hand) we have less time to stay in that house and we still like to live on hot dogs. . . . Would you believe that a hot dog is still my favorite food? If I had a choice between a steak and a hot dog, why I'd take the hot dog.*

# Tammy Wynette Collector's Guide

| YEAR | ALBUM | LABEL |
|------|-------|-------|
| 1967 | Your Good Girl's Gonna Go Bad | Epic |
| 1967 | My Elusive Dreams (with David Houston) | Epic |
| 1968 | Take Me to Your World/I Don't Wanna Play House | Epic |
| 1968 | D-I-V-O-R-C-E | Epic |
| 1969 | Stand By Your Man | Epic |
| 1969 | Inspiration | Epic |
| 1969 | Run Angel Run (soundtrack) | Epic |
| 1969 | Tammy's Greatest Hits | Epic |
| 1970 | The Ways to Love a Man | Epic |
| 1970 | Tammy's Touch | Epic |
| 1970 | The World of Tammy Wynette | Epic |
| 1970 | The First Lady | Epic |
| 1970 | Christmas with Tammy | Epic |
| 1971 | We Sure Love Each Other | Epic |
| 1971 | Tammy's Greatest Hits Volume II | Epic |
| 1971 | We Go Together (with George Jones) | Epic |
| 1972 | Bedtime Story | Epic |
| 1972 | My Man | Epic |
| 1973 | The First Songs of the First Lady | Epic |
| 1973 | Kids Say the Darndest Things | Epic |
| 1974 | Another Lonely Song | Epic |
| 1974 | Woman to Woman | Epic |
| 1975 | Greatest Hits Volume III | Epic |
| 1975 | I Still Believe in Fairy Tales | Epic |
| 1976 | Till I Can Make It On My Own | Epic |
| 1976 | Let's Get Together You and Me | Epic |
| 1977 | One of a Kind | Epic |
| 1977 | George and Tammy's Greatest Hits (with George Jones) | Epic |
| 1978 | Womanhood | Epic |
| 1978 | Greatest Hits Volume IV | Epic |
| 1979 | Just Tammy | Epic |

| YEAR | ALBUM | LABEL |
|---|---|---|
| 1980 | Only Lonely Sometimes | Epic |
| 1980 | Together Again (with George Jones) | Epic |
| 1981 | You Brought Me Back | Epic |
| 1981 | Encore | Epic |
| 1982 | Soft Touch | Epic |
| 1983 | Good Love and Heartbreak | Epic |
| 1983 | Even the Strong Get Lonely | Epic |

| YEAR | SINGLE | LABEL | C&W | POP |
|---|---|---|---|---|
| 1966 | Apartment Number 9 | Epic | | |
| 1967 | Your Good Girl's Gonna Go Bad | Epic | * | |
| 1967 | My Elusive Dreams (with David Houston) | Epic | | x |
| 1967 | I Don't Wanna Play House | Epic | * | |
| 1967 | Take Me To Your World | Epic | * | |
| 1967 | It's All Over (with David Houston) | Epic | | |
| 1968 | D-I-V-O-R-C-E | Epic | * | x |
| 1968 | Stand By Your Man | Epic | * | x |
| 1969 | Singing My Song | Epic | * | x |
| 1969 | The Ways to Love a Man | Epic | * | x |
| 1970 | I'll See Him Through (with David Houston) | Epic | * | x |
| 1970 | He Loves Me All the Way | Epic | * | x |
| 1970 | Run Woman Run | Epic | * | x |
| 1970 | The Wonders You Perform | Epic | * | |
| 1970 | One Happy Christmas | Epic | | |
| 1971 | We Sure Can Love Each Other | Epic | * | |
| 1971 | Good Lovin' (Makes It Right) | Epic | * | |
| 1972 | Bedtime Story | Epic | * | x |

* Smash Hit
X Crossover to Pop

| YEAR | SINGLE | LABEL | C&W | POP |
|------|--------|-------|-----|-----|
| 1972 | Reach Out Your Hand | Epic | * | |
| 1972 | My Man (Understands) | Epic | * | |
| 1972 | Till I Get It Right | Epic | * | |
| 1973 | Kids Say the Darndest Things | Epic | * | x |
| 1973 | Another Lonely Song | Epic | * | |
| 1974 | Woman to Woman | Epic | * | |
| 1975 | (You Make Me Want To Be) A Mother | Epic | * | |
| 1975 | I Still Believe in Fairy Tales | Epic | | |
| 1976 | Till I Can Make It On My Own | Epic | * | x |
| 1976 | You and Me | Epic | * | |
| 1977 | Southern California (with George Jones) | Epic | | |
| 1977 | Let's Get Together (One Last Time) | Epic | * | |
| 1977 | One of a Kind | Epic | * | |
| 1978 | I'd Like To See Jesus (On the Midnight Special) | Epic | | |
| 1978 | Womanhood | Epic | * | |
| 1979 | They Call It Making Love | Epic | * | |
| 1979 | No One Else in the World | Epic | * | |
| 1980 | He Was There (When I Needed You) | Epic | | |
| 1980 | Starting Over | Epic | | |
| 1980 | A Pair of Old Sneakers | Epic | | |
| 1980 | Cowboys Don't Shoot Straight (Like They Used To) | Epic | | |
| 1981 | Crying in the Rain | Epic | * | |
| 1982 | Another Chance | Epic | * | |
| 1982 | A Good Night's Love | Epic | * | |
| 1982 | You Still Get To Me in My Dreams | Epic | | |
| 1983 | I Just Heard a Heart Break (And I'm So Afraid It's Mine) | Epic | | |
| 1983 | Unwed Fathers | Epic | | |
| 1983 | Still in the Ring | Epic | | |

* Smash Hit
X Crossover to Pop

**236**

# Bibliography

Caress, Jay. *Hank Williams, Country Music's Tragic King.* New York: Stein and Day, 1975.

Carpozi, George. *The Johnny Cash Story.* New York: Pyramid Books, 1970.

Cash, Johnny. *Man in Black.* New York: Warner Books, 1975.

Flippo, Chet. *Your Cheatin' Heart.* New York: Simon & Schuster, 1981.

Gillet, Charlie. *The Sound of the City.* New York: Outerbridge & Dientsfrey, 1970.

Lynn, Loretta, with George Vecsey. *Coal Miner's Daughter.* New York: Warner Books, 1976.

Malone, Bill C. *Country Music U.S.A.* Austin: University of Texas Press, 1968.

Malone, Bill C., and Judith McCulloh, eds. *The Stars of Country Music.* New York: Avon Books, 1976.

Marcus, Greil. *Mystery Train.* New York: Signet Books/New American Library, 1976.

Palmer, Robert. *Jerry Lee Lewis Rocks!* New York: Delilah Books, 1981.

Scobey, Lola. *Willie Nelson, Country Outlaw.* New York: Zebra Books, 1982.

Shestack, Melvin. *The Country Music Encyclopedia.* New York: Thomas Y. Crowell Co., 1974.

Tosches, Nick. *Hellfire, The Jerry Lee Lewis Story.* New York: Dell Trade Paperbacks, 1982.

Whitburn, Joel. Record Research, based on *Billboard* magazine, 1949–1982.

Williams, Roger. *Sing a Sad Song; The Life of Hank Williams.* Garden City: Doubleday, 1970.

# Index

**238**

## About the Author

Gene Busnar is a musician, songwriter, and the author of the books, *It's Rock 'N' Roll, Superstars of Rock,* and *Careers in Music.* He is currently working on two upcoming Messner books, *More Superstars of Rock* and *The Rhythm & Blues Story.*